CW00326651

TELLING TALES

Further glimpses of Coventry Women

by

THE WOMEN'S RESEARCH GROUP

Published by The Women's Research Group
First Edition 2003

ISBN 0-9540604-2-3

Members of the group involved in writing this book.

JEAN APPLETON
ANGELA ATKIN
CHRISTINE BROMLEY
JUNE HILL
LYNN HOCKTON

Other books in this series

REDRESSING THE BALANCE
HURDY GURDY DAYS
KEEPING THE BALANCE

Cover photograph of The Land Army Girls.
Margaret Gamble is seated on the right.

Printed by V & J System Printers - 024 7671 5428

November 2003

Introduction

When the Women's Research Group was formed in 1998 to record the history of Coventry women, its members looked no further than completing its first book, 'Redressing the Balance,' published in 1999. Since then the work of the group has continued with two more books 'Hurdy Gurdy Days' and 'Keeping the Balance,' both published in 2001. The aims of the group are still the same, to research and record the contribution that women have made to the life of Coventry in the twentieth century.

This fourth book has moved on from the usual formula of individual profiles, to encompass the activities of groups, charities and organisations involving women. Those exclusively concerned with women, such as the Suffragettes, the Women's Land Army and the National Women's Register; to charities like the Coventry Stroke Group, which is equally concerned with men and the Moose Ladies, a section of the Loyal Order of Moose. The individuals are still there, from Muriel Hind, the first woman to take part in competitive motorcycle racing at the beginning of the twentieth century, to Miranda Aston, a thoroughly modern woman production engineer, at the end. There is something of interest to all who value Coventry and its women.

Acknowledgements

The Women's Research Group would like to thank the following organisations and individuals for their help in preparing this book.

Local Studies, Central Library, Coventry for their assistance in research.

The Museum of British Road Transport, especially Barry Collins for his help in research, and for their permission to reproduce the photograph of Muriel Hind.

The Coventry Building Society Charitable Foundation for permission to reproduce the photograph of Mary Hart.

Ulli Ull for permission to reproduce her photograph of Miranda Aston.

Individuals who have supplied information and photographs of themselves or relatives.

The Suffragettes.

The middle of the 19th century saw one of the most dramatic changes in the British economy as the rapid industrialisation of Britain drastically altered the fortunes and lives of its citizens. As the owners of the mills and factories gained in wealth and power, steamrollering their mass-produced goods onto and into the lives of the middle class, there were those who began to feel that this roller coaster economy, propelled by men for men, was giving men greater power than ever before.

With the ability to build and furnish their homes to a fine degree, many men now saw their wives as keepers of the home and family standards and supporters of their role as the head of the family. Economic power by men was aided by the legal profession who gave no property rights to married women, despite what wealth they may have brought to the marriage. It was in this climate of ruthless capitalism that the powerlessness felt by women at this time began to emerge and slowly be heard. In time this quiet first voicing of dissatisfaction would grow and feed into a mass movement, which would dominate society and politics into the next century.

The movement, which became known as the suffragettes, began with small groups of women from mainly new industrialised cities and towns, voicing resentment against the inequality of the political system. These 'angels of the hearth' resented their allotted place and felt their contribution to the home needed to be recognised in the national sphere. These small informal groups began to get organised. In time they would become more vociferous and, in some areas of the country, more violent. But those early stirrings were the bedrock on which the movement progressed.

And Coventry was one of those places where those feelings were being expressed in a formal way. Long before Emmeline Pankhurst formed her militant group, the Women's Social and Political Union in 1903, Coventry women had a local branch of the Women's Suffrage Society from 1868. It was not until 1897 that the National Union of Women's Suffrage Society was formed with 5 branches, the largest being Birmingham.

It was to be the early part of the 20th century which was to see the most of militant action by the suffragette movement, and it can be no coincidence that the involvement of the Pankhurst women helped to bring this about.

In 1907 Emmeline and Christobel had resigned from the Independent Labour Party as they disagreed on its policy towards emancipation. Ironically, their own leadership of the WSPU at that time had caused problems. Some members felt it was becoming too autocratic and had left to form the

Women's Freedom League. However, in 1908 when Prime Minister Asquith proposed the Women's Suffragette Amendment, all rifts seem to have been set aside and 300,000 women demonstrated against it.

The rising militant action at this time meant that many of the women were to experience time in prison for their actions. Stone throwing at the windows of government buildings became a common form of protest, and although this behaviour was less usual in the provinces, the effects of it were noticeable.

Miss Alice Lea gained public recognition in the Coventry local newspapers for her actions as a militant protester in London. Miss Lea, whose family connections included the car manufacturing firm, Lea Francis, received an overwhelming reception on her return from a month's stay at Holloway Prison. Far from condemning her stone throwing, she was positively applauded for her militant stance and press coverage of the event seemed to suggest that the movement was now being taken very seriously.

The welcoming speech given by the Reverend P.E.T. Widdrington, showed full support for these more militant actions.

'The WSPU was a militant society; it was a society of extremists, of people who were going to get what they wanted, and were going to use strong means to get what they wanted. There were and had been heaps of "ladylike" societies in existence for the purpose of obtaining the franchise for women, but until the WSPU came along the women's movement did not count in English political life.'

Another member of the welcoming party, Mr J.C. Smythe, MA, of Bradford College, also gave a lengthy address on "The Militant Tactics" and gained much applause when he referred to the WSPU saying, 'Theirs was the only practical movement there has been for the last fifty years, and that was the reason why it had his own individual support, and would do to the end.'

From notes written by Miss Lea we have her own personal account of the events. It seemed that the gentility accorded her as a respectable middle class woman degenerated with her stay in prison.

'Every kindness was shown to us by the police and friends and sympathisers; flowers, fruit and a farewell luncheon were generously lavished upon us; ..... For the last hour.... we were separated from friends and locked in cells to await our removal. There we found two women prisoners who, for small sums, could be released - this was collected among us and they went away rejoicing.

"Gaily we go to prison," has been truly said, but only those who have realised it and know how the courage that has been enough to keep a smiling face and a brave heart until then, is strained to breaking pitch at the first experience of degradation the drive in the Black Maria on reaching Holloway Gaol we again had long hours of waiting. In cells with a seat and an air space for one person, four together were kept waiting until we felt light-headed with fatigue. For the climax of that day's degradation, the donning of the criminal's dress. I refrain from going into details they are revolting we were told to undress completely, have a bath and put on prison dress. Suffice it to say that in the presence of wardresses and other prisoners we were stripped of all our clothes and possessions and from baskets around took the felon's garments we were henceforth to wear. It was the acme of gratuitous insult nothing mattered after that.'

Not only city women were prepared to take action. In the nearby village of Berkswell, Lettice Annie Floyd, a member of a substantial local family who owned several farms and numerous cottages, and the youngest daughter of William and Alison Floyd, had also been an active supporter. She had on one occasion taken a stone from Berkswell to London, wrapped up in her pocket-handkerchief, which she threw through the window of No. 10 Downing Street. She was imprisoned several times but continued to support the cause. She was also a friend of Mrs Emmeline Pankhurst who used to visit her at Berkswell.

Of course these militant actions were seized upon by the newspapers and the press covered the progress or otherwise of the suffragettes regularly. However, their treatment of the subject varied considerably and the Coventry Graphic in 1912 gave a serious, straight forward account of a suffragette meeting held at the Bath's Assembly Rooms. The meeting was addressed by Mrs Pankhurst and support for the cause was voiced by a Mr D.M. Mason MP, who felt that the suffragette cause was winning.

However, Mr Harry Tate, a comedian, was given half a page to write an article in which he pondered on the domestic outcome of women having the vote in an entirely facetious tone.

'Of course, there will be a law, when women vote, that all engaged men must wear an engagement ring, just to check their flirtations, and if such fellows do get caught philandering I tremble to think what the legal penalty may be. This question of flirtations between engaged or married men and single women is sure to attract a lot of attention when women come to power, and the great question to decide will be whether to punish the poor weak man who flirts or the bold bachelor girl who encourages him most severely. Elections will probably be fought over this problem, passionate speeches be delivered, and bad eggs be exchanged between the two parties before the matter is settled......... There will be no such things as rowdy husbands when women have the vote. You cannot get rowdy on lemonade, and that is about the only drink you will be allowed unless you get a doctor's certificate to say that your health need a little stimulant.'

To remedy this situation the Graphic did allow lengthy, serious consideration of the matter. In May 1912 a full column was given to an article "In praise of the Window Smashers" in which a 'Miss Elizabeth Robins, the most brilliant literary exponent of the tactics of the militant Suffragettes' was quoted as saying 'she was full of "thankfulness" that, in spite of provocation women so far have not, in their struggle for freedom, emulated the more violent deeds of men...... Women, says Miss Robins are kept closer to reality and common sense than men but she exults in the success of the militant tactics in doing away with the tolerant amusement with which the claims of women were formerly regarded....... Stone throwing has not only broken windows: it has broken apathy,' In the same article it is recorded that support for the tactics was now coming from establishment male figures. 'Mr Gladstone put his views in these terms: I am sorry to say that if no instructions have ever been addressed in political crisis to the people of this country, except to hate violence and love order and exercise patience, the liberties of this country would never have been attained.'

In November 1912 the paper carried correspondence from two women writers. On November 2nd the first writer put the question of emancipation in context and argued that what would have made our grandmothers stand back in horror and amazement was now acceptable. 'A few years back the idea of a woman earning her own living was looked upon with contempt.' However, she is aware that equality in the workplace has not been achieved and states that 'Now, when the women are at work, because they are the weaker sex, they are given the lighter work, which means lighter pay.' She finally acknowledges that 'there are many difficulties regarding details as to family life, etc. ....but when obligation leaves no choice it is amazing to find how the seeming mountains become mole heaps. Women are as loyal and patriotic as men; surely they would not like to see England ruined. Let us give them a chance then, before we are too hasty and rash about the absurdness of the question.'

But even this cautious and well-researched piece was still received with indignation. A letter to the editor of the Coventry Graphic, November 16th in answer to the previous writer declared herself 'to the contrary' and felt that 'the vast majority of women would prefer to be as their grandmothers and great grandmothers of years ago.' Indeed the writer seems to imply that the there

4

movement itself is responsible for wider changes in society. 'In these days of hobble skirts, and even such things as harem skirts, women are indeed becoming out of all proportion, but I will point out that this is not followed up by all women, and I am glad to say that there are still some of us with a sense of modest dignity...... Now why not let us be content with the numerous privileges we already have, for remember everything cometh to him that waits.'

But wait the suffragettes would not. These years running up to the First World War saw increasing violence. Further afield in the north of England a railway was set on fire, the Rokeby Venus at the National Gallery in London was defaced, and a dead kitten was flung at an anti-franchise speaker in Bristol. Even in Coventry militant 'suffragetism' was on the prowl, as can be seen by a report of February 1st, 1914 when 'destructive fluid was dropped into the letter box at the General Post Office and damage was done to at least two articles that had been posted.' The following month did not see any let up of this behaviour and interruptions by suffragettes at a meeting of the Labour Party, was not seen to advance their cause. There was a fear that this new mood of agitation would put back the cause as it was felt that 'if women were given the vote, the present agitators would assume the leadership of the feminist movement, and their present attitude and actions do not inspire confidence in their ability to undertake the role.'

Indeed, their militant tactics had entered into the common parlance. The Reverend J Samuel Hughes, former pastor of the Webster Street Baptist Church in Coventry had caused consternation and had suffered a breakdown while travelling from Shrewsbury to Llandrindod Wells. Declaring he would have a "suffrage night" he then smashed 43 windows at Shrewsbury station with stones. The police surgeon, however, declared him unfit to plead.

But this time the movement had mistimed their tactics. Another and more pressing worry was beginning to eclipse the country. The rumblings from abroad were growing louder and in a far-flung country a bomb was thrown at a member of a long reigning dynasty. The problems of the women's movement began to assume less urgency as the government and the country faced up to war with Germany.

In the next four years women were to prove their worthiness as they took on the challenges thrown up by a horrific and devastating war.

Almost unnoticed the 1918 Bill was passed, which gave the vote to women over 30 and householders, wives of householders, occupiers of property with a rent of £5 or more per annum and graduates of British the long universities. In 1928 all women over the age of 21 were given the vote. This was possibly in recognition of their work during the war years, but it would be hard to imagine the passing of this Bill without the long and arduous campaign, that had begun in the closing years of the 19th century, and had ended as a highly organised and determined movement of women.

Acknowledgements
Thank you to Miss Norma Lea for her help and supplying notes about her aunt.

Bibliography
Coventry Graphic 1912 - 1918.
Midland Daily Telegraph 1913, 1939.
The Women's Suffrage Movement, UCL Press 1999.
Berkswell Through a Looking Glass, D.E. Gibbs.
Deeds not Words, Emmeline Pankhurst, Leader of the Militant Suffragettes - June Purvis History Today May 2002.

~~~~~~

Muriel Hind

' "I saw a lady on one of them motor cycles this morning" remarked one man to the other. "Ladies don't ride them things," was the chilling response. "They do; for I saw one of them this morning," the first man persisted. But his companion was not convinced. "Get out man," he rejoined aggravatingly, "you either went to bed too late or got up too early." ' *The Motor News.*

'We were rather pleasantly surprised one day last week in Coventry, to see a tall but rather slender lady emerge from the yard of one of the hotels wheeling a motor cycle. Almost without effort she slipped into the saddle and pedalling firmly, but not laboriously, for a few seconds, she started the engine and soon disappeared from view, exhibiting a remarkable control of her machine.'   *The Motor Cycle.*

In both of these cases the lady referred to was Agnes Muriel Hind.

Muriel Hind was born in the latter part of the nineteenth century into a Dorset county family. Sadly she was orphaned at the age of seven years and so was brought up by relatives. The most usual form of transport in those days was the horse, but by the turn of the century the bicycle was becoming ever more popular.

Miss Hind derived great enjoyment riding along the country lanes on her pedal bicycle. It was on one of these occasions, when she was struggling up a hill against a strong wind, that she was overtaken by her brother on a motor-bicycle. He stopped and gave her a tow home. So was born Muriel Hind's desire to have a motor-bicycle of her own. We must remember that this was the turn of the century and the idea of a woman riding a motor-bicycle was regarded as 'disgraceful and unladylike'.

So Miss Hind thought it more diplomatic to await her twenty-first birthday before acquiring her first machine, and in 1902, after consultation with her brother, she ordered a 2 h.p., gear-driven, Singer with the engine enclosed in the back wheel.

As she had some experience of driving a car and also riding a bicycle it took no time at all for her to master her new machine, travelling, in fact, twenty-five miles on her first day. It did, however, take a little longer for her to learn the niceties of riding.

Her first machine was followed by a 2½ h.p. gear-driven Singer, and then a 3 h.p. chain-driven Singer. As Singer motor-bicycles were made in Coventry it necessitated several visits by Miss Hind to the city.

In the April of 1905 she joined the Motor Cycling Club, and entered her first competition on October 7th of that year. This competition was for the Albert Brown Trophy and Miss Hind's entry was in a Singer Tri-car. The event consisted of a 150 mile run, followed by a hill climb, a speed test and a brake test. As the only lady competitor, although she did not win, she was awarded a special certificate, for: "She showed remarkable physical endurance, good nerve and judgement."

In 1906 she entered the London to Edinburgh run, again in a Singer Tri-car, and won the gold medal. Of the fifteen competitors who started the run only three finished it.

With the same car and lady passenger she entered the six days run from Land's End to John O' Groats, and this time won a bronze medal.

The 1908 January Quarterly Trial of the A-C.U. was run in very bad weather, but Muriel Hind made the fastest time on both of the hill tests. This year also saw her again win a gold medal in the London to Edinburgh run. She was eventually to win five gold medals for this event.

After the Singer machines Muriel Hind had a 5 h.p. Roc, which was specially built for her. But following this she began to favour Rex machines, which were also Coventry designed and built. This association with the Rex Company was to bring her into contact with Richard (Dick) Lord; the gentleman who was eventually to become her husband.

In 1910 Miss Hind had entered the Coventry Motor Club's annual open hill climb on Willersey Hill, Gloucestershire, but unfortunately her Rex machine was not ready in time. Undaunted she borrowed the Rex machine belonging to E.A. Gorton who had achieved the fastest time for the run and beat his time by two and three-fifths seconds. Because it was not her machine the time could not be officially recognised. However, she was later presented with a silver cup, by the club, to remind her of her achievement.

As early as 1903 Muriel Hind had written articles on Motor Cycling for Ladies but it was not until 1910 that she persuaded the Motor Cycling magazine to let her do a fortnightly feature 'The Lady Motorcyclist'. This collaboration lasted until 1914.

Her articles covered many aspects of her sport, not least clothing. Women were not allowed to dress as men in those days, so the normal habit of a lady motorcyclist was a long tweed skirt, laced-up knee boots, a large hat held on with a scarf tied under the chin and a light-weight waterproof overall in case of bad weather.

Because of her interest in the sport she persuaded many manufacturers to make machines especially for ladies. Her views and opinions were taken into account when the Rex Company made their first ladies' bike. She test-drove many of the ladies' machines herself.

Her articles included many amusing accounts of her motoring experiences.

Muriel Hind had joined the Motor Cycling Club in 1905 and she retained this membership until 1950 when she was elected an Honorary Life Member. This was indeed a great honour, for by 1908 the MCC had refused to take any more women members and it was not until the early 1950s that they again opened their doors to female membership.

To be a member of the Association of Pioneer Motor Cyclists one must have ridden before 1904. As Miss Hind had obtained her first motor cycle driving licence in 1904 she qualified for membership she was their only lady member. In 1931 she was elected a Life-Member of this Association.

Her competitive career came to an end in 1912 when she married Mr Richard Lord of the Rex Company.

As a lady riding and competing during the early 1900s Muriel Hind had to face incredulity, scepticism and prejudice.

Having made up her mind that she was going to ride motor cycles she showed great single mindedness in her determination to follow her star. Never afraid to speak her mind she was always ready to promote her sport in a positive and polite manner. She never missed an opportunity to encourage other women to take up the sport.

During her years of riding she toured many thousands of miles. She seemed to have no fear of travelling on her own and found most people, if curious, were only too willing to help her if and when a problem arose. Not only a rider, she was also able to deal with most of her mechanical problems as well.

Despite having to give up competition in 1912 her interest and participation in riding and driving mechanical machines never diminished.

For over forty years she lived, with her family, in Wall Hill Hall in Corley until her death on May 3rd 1956.

She was deeply mourned by her husband and her son, but she was also mourned by all pioneer motor cyclists. She was a first the first woman to ride a motor cycle and the first woman to ride a motor cycle competitively a real pioneer.

***I must thank Mr Barry Collins of the Coventry Motor Museum
for his invaluable help.***

Acknowledgements:
> *The Motor Cycling Magazine*
> *The Motor News*
> *The Motor Cycle*
> *The Motor*
> *Autocar*
> *The Coventry Standard Newspaper*

> *I have endeavoured to identify all my sources. If I have inadvertently omitted any, please accept my apologies.*

The Women's Land Army.

The Women's Land Army was made up of girls from every walk of life. The first WLA was set up in great haste in 1917, as food was scarce. There were three major factors which contributed to the shortage, the loss of shipping in the Atlantic, carrying food from America, the men who usually worked on the land being away fighting in the war and the general decline in farming practice.

Many women patriotically applied to join the WLA; they were milking cows, driving tractors, field workers, carters, shepherds, ploughing and thatching roofs. Their efforts proved to be outstanding. Although the general consensus of the farmers was that women would not be able to do the work of men, they were proved wrong.

Then again in 1939 the women were needed on the land for the Second World War. In Europe women had always worked alongside the farmers doing all kinds of manual work, but the English women only did light jobs like collecting the eggs, feeding the calves and pigs and tending to the kitchen garden, they soon learnt other aspects of farming. They were also employed in large private gardens if their work would help feed the country. Most of the women were naïve with regards to farming practice, who had previously been in all kinds of occupations.

The Government made the decision to approach Lady Denman; a pioneer in the Women's Institute movement. She came from a wealthy family, the daughter of Viscount Cowdray. Although from a privileged background, she worked most of her life campaigning for better living conditions, better education and better medical facilities for the working class. She had helped previously with setting up the Women's Land Army in the First World War. She was able to draw on people from the Women's Institute to help form a committee and to set up Land Army Committees in each county. Using the Women's Institute members lists she wrote to the women she had chosen to be chairman of each county. Lady Denman initially had to really fight for a minimum wage of twenty-eight shillings (£1.40) a week for the land girls, later it was increased. For girls living in a billet fourteen shillings (70 pence) was deducted from their wages for their keep.

Their uniforms had to be practical for use in all weather conditions; fawn corduroy knee breeches, matching aertex shirts, a green and red striped tie with the motif WLA in yellow letters and a V- necked pullover, also a "pork pie" hat with a WLA badge and a green felt arm-band. They had thick knee-length woollen socks that were turned down over the hem of the breeches and stiff brown leather brogues or boots. In 1942 a fawn overcoat was introduced and in 1949 the "pork-pie" felt hat was replaced by a green beret. For their actual working clothes they had camel coloured dungarees, rubber boots, milking coat which was like a mackintosh and of course the well known head scarf.

At the start of clothing rationing each girl was ordered to give up 10 coupons straight away for uniform replacements. Because of the nature of their work the girls were given extra coupons to replace work clothing. Their woollen socks took a lot of darning and wore out quickly.

Later the Timber Corps was set up; these women were given a two to three week course at a training centre in the Forest of Dean. After training girls were placed either in a forest or at a sawmill, their wages were forty-five shillings (£2.25) a week.

There were many anomalies between the WLA and other women's services; for instance they never had the same benefits as the ATS or the WAAF they had to register themselves with local doctors whereas the other services were under constant medical supervision.

When a member of the WLA left she was allowed 20 to 35 clothing coupons, but no clothing allowance, whereas, the ATS got 160 coupons plus a clothing allowance of £12.10s (£12.50). If a girl in the WLA gave a week's notice to leave she did not receive any unemployment benefit, the ATS girls were paid demobilisation leave. The WLA were able to keep their overcoats provided they dyed them blue, they could also keep their shoes. The Prime Minister Mr Churchill announced to the House of Commons, that the WLA was to be recognised as an auxiliary arm of industry, so therefore no gratuities would be granted. Lady Denman was so disgusted with the government's decision that she resigned. Even after Lady Denman's resignation Queen Elizabeth the Queen Mother remained patron of the WLA.

After VJ Day girls did receive letters informing them that they could seek release from the WLA if they so wished. When the WLA was disbanded on the 30TH November 1950, many of the farmers who had been against the idea of women working on the land, were very sorry to see them go. The last job done by the WLA was to help eradicate the Colorado Beetle, which threatened to destroy the national potato crop. Many of the girls remained working on the land after it was disbanded.

What would have happened if these women had not worked on the land? Frequently enduring inferior lodgings, inadequate feeding and adverse weather conditions, either freezing cold or blistering hot. Obviously, the WLA should have received more appreciation.

Vera Hewitt.

Vera Vincent was born in the village of Piddlehinton, which is five miles from Dorchester, the daughter of a farmer. The farm was passed down to her father from her grandfather. The farmhouse had no electricity or running water so candles were used for lighting and water had to be fetched from a well.

She went to the village school (no longer a school, but the village hall). The children used to walk to school carrying their satchels on their backs with jam sandwiches and a bottle of milk, cold tea or lemonade. Walking to school, they sometimes had a tin, which they pushed along with a stick; the trick was to arrive at school without making a hole in it. She can remember the teacher taking the children into the playground to see the occasional aeroplane in the sky. There were very few cars on the road at this time and the children could hear them coming up the lane and they got really excited. The vicar had a car in the 1920s and if they saw him they would jump up and down waving at him.

Vera went to Sunday School, which was held in the morning and again in the afternoon. When the weather was cold they would stand around the iron stove to get some warmth. Christmas morning at church was always a treat as the children were given an orange. Each year they had a Sunday School outing to Weymouth.

When it was time for Vera to leave school she started thinking about what she wanted to do, it crossed her mind that maybe she would like to be a teacher, but unfortunately her mother became ill and there was a lot for her to do. Then war was declared and as there was a shortage of men to work on the land, (they had gone into the services); she started to work on her father's farm. Her main job was milking the cows; she says it took her ages before she became proficient at it. Later on her father bought a milking machine, he was the first farmer in the village to do so and Vera started using this. She could take it apart and put it together again, the reason for this was that the machine had to be thoroughly sterilised.

When the farm workers had gone into the forces Vera's father needed help on the farm and he applied to the Women's Land Army to try and recruit labour and was lucky enough to get two Land Girls. Both of these girls came from towns and they found the work very hard, but they appeared to enjoy it once they had settled in. The girls did not live at the farm but in a hostel, they did all kinds of work, threshing, ploughing and potato picking. During the threshing period there were a number of rats running about and the Land

Girls got used to killing them with their pitchforks. Unfortunately, one the Land Girls called Joan Davis, who came from London, met with an accident and was killed in 1943. She was sitting on a trailer, which was loaded with hay, the tractor was being driven by Vera's brother, and it skidded and the trailer overturned trapping the Land Army girl beneath it, she was only 20 years of age. The Coroner's Inquest recorded a verdict of Death by Misadventure; this was a sad time for all the people connected with the farm. German POWs who were billeted at Puddletown, Dorset, were driven to the farm each morning to work, picked up at night and taken back to their camp. Vera said that as soon as war was declared a big army camp was built in no time at all, this was situated between her farm and the village and both she and her friend used to take the dog for a walk and kept passing by the army base to see if they could see any soldiers. With all this happening their lives were transformed. When the American forces arrived Vera said it was the first time she had seen a coloured person. There were dances held in the village school and life began to change, it was never to be the same again. People got used to seeing army lorries trundling along the narrow country lanes. The families in the village did their best to make the soldiers welcome and would invite them into their homes. Vera's family had a piano, which her mother played, and the soldiers who were invited for tea or coffee gathered round the piano for a singsong.

One Sunday afternoon as Vera was going to get the cows in for milking, someone knocked on the farmhouse door, upon opening it, there were two British soldiers who asked if they could go into the farmyard as they needed worms to go fishing. Vera asked them where was their home town, one said Coventry and the other Leeds, after getting the worms they went off to fish. That evening the soldiers returned to the farmyard and shortly afterwards Vera arrived to see her mother standing at the door holding a bowl with trout in it, which had been given to her by the soldiers. The soldiers thanked Vera for the worms and told her that their regiment was leaving the camp the next day; they said they would have liked to do more fishing. Vera joked with them saying "If you come this way again, let me know and I will get the worms ready", the Coventry soldier said, "Who do I write to", Vera replied "Miss Vera, Piddlehinton, Dorset". Some weeks later she received a letter from Ray who was the one from Coventry, saying he and his friend would like to come and do more fishing and would she get the worms ready, which she did. When they arrived at the farm they said they were probably going to stay in the pub in the next village, but Vera's mother invited them to have the spare room and they took her up on her offer. Ray went several times on his own to fish, sometimes Vera would go in the evenings to the riverbank and they would walk back to the farm together. At other times they would walk to the next village for Ray to catch a bus to Salisbury and from there a train to his camp.

Yes, you have guessed it, from a jar of worms to romance. Ray was given embarkation leave and asked Vera if she would join him in Coventry to meet his parents who lived in Earlsdon Avenue and see the city. She took the train, which at that time was a long tedious journey and arrived at Coventry on a foggy, murky day. She really enjoyed her visit, but could not wait to get back to Dorset. Ray was away for a few years, but they wrote to each other regularly. A few years after he was demobbed, they were married and Vera moved to Coventry. This must have been hard for her to adjust to city life after living in a lovely Dorset village, she was very homesick and occasionally she and Ray went back to Piddlehinton for a weekend. Vera and Ray had eight children and they used to take them to Dorset for their summer holidays. She was not so lonely once she had the children as she met other mothers at the school and started to get involved in local activities. Ray hoped that when he retired they would leave Coventry and go and live in Dorset. Sadly, he passed away, so never had his wish. After this Vera had no inclination to leave Coventry, she has lived here since 1949, and has made many friends and found new interests to pursue.

Vera is a busy lady and is active in many groups such as The Creative Writers Group, Coventry Playwrights Group, drama groups, The Townswomen's Guild, and the W.O.W.W Group (What Older Women Want), which is involved in numerous activities. She has also written articles in various books, one in particular being 'Memories of Piddlehinton School in the 1920s and 1930s', as a former pupil. This is included in The Story of Piddlehinton, a Dorset Village History.

Vera may not be able to drive or use a computer, but she can milk cows, Can you?

The writer would like to thank Vera for letting her be interviewed.

Interview took place October 2003.

Celia Davies.

Celia was born in Bristol in June 1919. She was interested in joining the Wrens, but on listening to two girls talking on the radio about the Women's Land Army she wanted to learn more about this and do a her bit for her country, so she went along to the Labour Exchange to hear what they had to say. As she was frightened of cows it was suggested that she should join the Forestry Section of the WLA, this was different from the Timber Corps, so she enlisted.

From April until August 1941 she did her training at Parkend Forestry School in the Forest of Dean, Gloucestershire, where she was taught all about trees, saplings and the woodland. Whilst here a fire broke out in the woods, this was caused by bombs being dropped by enemy aircraft, the girls were called upon to get the fire under control, they had to use beaters, eventually the Army had to be called in to assist. The Forestry Girls were supplied with socks, shoes, army boots, two aertex shirts, dungarees, Wellington boots, breeches and a green jumper. After her training she was transferred to Colsterworth, a village off the Great North Road, Lincolnshire, where she worked in woodlands felling trees, and replacing them with new saplings. There was nothing wasted from the felled trees, the branches had to be stripped and given to the farmers to be used for hedging. They had to physically drag any dead trees out and saw them into 6ft lengths, then used 7lb axes to make them into stakes, which were taken to the beaches to be used to help stop invasions by the enemy. Dead wood (Cord Wood) had to be weighed in tons and lorries arrived to take it to be used in the munitions factories. She also waded in ditches to clear, drain and reclaim the land. The tools used were crosscut saws, axes, slashers and billhooks. Celia worked in Lincolnshire for twelve months. When they were working in the woods if they decided to have a sit down for a ten-minute break the birds always gave a warning if anybody was around, so the girls would get up and carry on with their jobs.

In the house where Celia was billeted in Colsterworth, there was only one tap for the kitchen sink. On Friday nights she had to go to the pump in the village to get the water for her bath, which she would have on Saturday. This was after she had got the fire going to heat the water, for both her bath and to do her washing. The out-house became her bathroom (Oh! for mod.cons).

In 1942/3 she moved to Hertfordshire and lived in a large house called Barns Lodge, but she was only there for six months. The house was then taken over by the Polish Army for its headquarters. Here she worked on different farms doing threshing, potato picking (which she has never forgotten) and setting out potatoes. Farmers always wanted the girls from the Forestry Section to work for them as they considered them to be hard workers and reliable. She drove a tractor, ploughed fields and reclaimed land. These tractors ran on paraffin and many times she had to take out the plugs and burn them to get rid of the excess oil and put them back into the engine before it would start. Chains would be put around shrubs and pulled out by the tractor and then the land ploughed.

On one occasion she volunteered to do a milk round, as the usual milk girl was taken ill. She had to harness the horse to attach it to the cart; she had never done this before, but soon learnt. She went to different houses and farms to deliver the milk which was served out of churns. At one place the farmer was a widower with a son who was mentally a bit slow and Celia made them a drink of tea but could not find any milk in the kitchen, she told Tom the farmer and he said, "Tell Joe," which she did. He took the cups and squirted the milk straight into the cups from the cows udders. She said that the majority of the farmers' wives whom she called upon were very kind to her and would frequently offer her a drink and a piece of cake. (Oh! to be a milkmaid).

Whilst in Gloucestershire, in May 1944, Celia was involved in an accident, damaging her foot. She was driving a three-ton lorry, along the road when a convoy of American Army lorries carrying explosives passed her by going in the opposite direction. Suddenly one pulled out of line and crashed into her lorry. She spent some time in hospital, but later returned to the Forestry Section.

She then went to Pendley Manor, near Tring, in Hertfordshire; this was a big house on an estate owned by a Mrs Williams. There were about 30/40 girls working doing different jobs on the farm, here Celia did threshing, (whilst the rats and mice were fleeing from the crops), she also did other farm work. On one occasion all the girls were covered in spots, the doctor was called and he diagnosed Scabies. He called for a nurse and the girls had to stand naked in a hall whilst she pasted them with ointment (no modesty here). Celia wrote to her mother telling her she had scabies and she thought it was dreadful and said "It must have been caused by dirt." Of course it was very dirty and dusty work doing the threshing.

At one of the billets the girls were only allowed 5 inches of water in which to bath and there was a black painted line around the bath marking the exact measure. There were three in a bath scrubbing each others backs (again no modesty here), after their bath they had to wash their clothes in the same water.

Celia moved to Gloucestershire late in 1943, where she drove girls by lorry to the farms to do their work, later she became forewoman. She also drove Italian and German P.O.Ws to work in the sugar beet fields. At one time the Italians refused to get into the back of her lorry (perhaps it was because she was a female). Some of the young German P.O.Ws spat at the land girls feet, these girls had to work alongside them. If the girls became friendly with them they were dismissed. The girls also worked with civilian prisoners and conscientious objectors, which of course could not have been pleasant.

At Pendley Manor the Army were billeted in the stables and occasionally ENSA entertained the soldiers and the girls were invited to the concerts to watch such stars as Norman Evans of "Over the garden wall" fame. Sometimes the girls went to dances at the American Bases; lorries would be sent to take them and return them to their billet. When in Tring, Herefordshire a Sergeant Major taught the Women's Land Army how to march; he did this in the hopes that they would look smart when marching with the troops. At Bovingdon, Hertfordshire, the girls were invited to an American Air force dance. Celia said they always had excellent bands, but the dance floor was rough concrete. On one occasion she wore the soles of her shoes away and on another they were given no food and were starving. When they got back to their hostel and told the women in charge she made them a hot drink and gave them a piece of cake. She then wrote to the Commanding Officer at the base complaining about the lack of food. From then on it was dunkin' doughnuts and Spam sandwiches (How lucky can you get!!!).

The girls worked very long hours, their wake up call was at 5.30 and started work at 7 o'clock. When harvesting, because of double summertime, it was nothing for them to be working up until 11 pm and then have to cycle a few miles to their hostel, have a bath and up early the next day to start again. There were strict rules regarding what time they had to be back at the hostel if they went out. In winter it was 10 pm and a late pass 10.30 pm and summer 10.30 pm and the last pass 11 pm

Celia says the girls were allowed two free travel passes a year. She used to travel overnight by train to her home in Bristol, at the various stations she drank tea from jam jars as the cups were only for the use of officers.

Celia says that being in the Forestry Section was an experience she was glad to have had, feeling she had done something for her country. She also said that the companionship was wonderful.

She has lived in Coventry for twenty-nine years.

Interviewed June 2003.

Margaret Gamble

Margaret Gamble, was thrilled to be on the team preparing for the grand opening of the new Owen Owen store, Coventry in 1937. She worked there very happily until the blitz of 14th November 1940 destroyed the building. With so many of her relatives and friends in the forces she felt she should be doing her bit towards the war effort. She decided to volunteer for the Women's Land Army in 1941, despite have no experience of animals or the countryside.

Some recruits had preliminary training at agricultural college, but Margaret found herself kitted out with her uniform and sent off to a dairy farm on the outskirts of Stratford-upon-Avon to learn on the job. She billeted with a farm labourer and his wife and was treated very well. Her first morning began by being woken at 4.30am; after washing and dressing she was sent off to the field with only a cup of tea to sustain her. Breakfast was not eaten until after the early milking was completed. Across the fields she went feeling half asleep and full of trepidation.

When she arrived the cows were already waiting by the mobile milking parlour. She was shocked when told to wash the cow's udders before attaching the teats to the milking machine. She was shown how to use the machine, but it was far from easy. She thought she was doing fine getting three in place, but when she tried to attach the fourth they all fell off and she had to start all over again. With practice she did master the technique and quite enjoyed the hand stripping, extracting the last of the milk by hand after the machine was removed, except when a cow flicked a dirty tail around her ear. Occasionally she helped out in the dairy, although she was frightened of the sterilizer when it built up steam and thought it would blow up at any moment and take her with it.

She did a variety of jobs around the farm, such as hedging and ditching, hoeing and thinning out the crops. Her pet hate was cutting kale on cold, frosty mornings and the backbreaking potato picking, especially when it was wet, with mud sticking to her boots. In these conditions the girls wore sacks over their heads and shoulders, with the point sticking up to give them some protection from the rain. She thought they must have looked like monks from a bygone age. She should have been issued with a waterproof coat, but never did get it.

The Land Girls worked very hard at all times for very little money, as the cost of their billet came out of the basic pay. There was very little free time to visit relatives as there was always another task waiting to be done. Harvest time was a particularly demanding time of year, when everyone was needed to put in the maximum effort. Raking the chaff from the thresher was a terrible job for it went everywhere, in their eyes, up their noses and down their shirts. Rats and mice ran everywhere and they were expected to kill them with whatever implement came to hand. Amongst the girls there was much teasing, many laughs and a great camaraderie.

The river Avon ran alongside the field near Margaret's billet. She thought she was dreaming one day when her fiancé suddenly appeared from nowhere with a broad grin on his face. He had hired a boat in Stratford and rowed along the river until he found her. He was in the forces and only had an hour free to see her. He often popped up unexpectedly at various places around the farm, before he was posted to North Africa. The locals nicknamed him Jack-in-the-box for his antics.

After two and a half years she was moved to Astley Court, near Fillongley and put in charge of several girls from the Birmingham area. The house either belonged to or was requisitioned by the Standard Motor Company for the duration of the war. The Land Girls billeted there were taken by van each morning to the Standard factory in Tile Hill to cultivate the land at the side of the site. They grew vegetables for the factory canteen. Sometimes they worked in the walled garden at Astley Court.

After suffering with pain in her right side for some time, she asked to move to lighter work. She transferred to a nursery near Elmdon (Birmingham) Airport, growing tomatoes, and later to another in Tile Hill, Coventry. The pain in her side grew worse and turned out to be her appendix that was causing the trouble. She was hospitalised and it was removed. By the time she had recovered the war was virtually over, it was June 1945 and she was discharged from the Women's Land Army. She married her Jack-in the-box in October 1945 when he was on leave, although he was sent away for another six months afterwards, before he was finally discharged.

Thank you to Margaret for her memories and help in compiling this article.

Beryl Hutchinson nee Allcoat.

Beryl was born in Arley, Nuneaton, Warwickshire. Just after her seventeenth birthday she decided to join the Women's Land Army. The country needed more food production, as the farm workers were away at war, so she looked at the prospect of joining. She went to Birmingham for her medical and was deemed fit. After this she went to Leamington Spa to collect her uniform.

She travelled with other girls by train to Studley, Warwickshire, where they were met by a person in a Land Rover and were transported to their accommodation, a hostel called Oak Trees. She had six weeks training at Quinny's, which was a big dairy farm situated at Sambourne, near Studley, (that handled all the Land Girls training). The girls were split into groups. Beryl was to learn about all aspects of dairy work, hand and machine milking and also the bottling of the milk, for two weeks, getting up at 4 am and cycling to Samborne. Then it was her turn to learn how to look after poultry, for another two weeks. The next two weeks was learning about all kinds of fieldwork. After training, if you passed all the tests you were awarded your Oak Leaves, which was a metal badge. Her wages were the magnificent amount of £3.00 per week

It was now time for the girls to move on to work on various farms. Her first placement was at Grange Farm, Henley in Arden, Warwickshire, which was a very superior farm. She worked there with another girl called Mary Groves and they had a wonderful time. Mr Saunders the farmer, treated them like his own family and even allowed them his daughters school room for their private use. In winter Mr Saunders would have a big fire going and would use bellows if the fire was not roaring. They ate with the family, having the best of everything. The farmer had two daughters and whilst Beryl was at the farm one of his daughters, Jean, who was an officer in the WRNS came home on leave from Mombassa. The eldest daughter Audrey often went to the RAF officers' club at Stratford upon Avon, and sometimes arrived back at the farm at 3am to throw gravel from the drive up to Beryl's window so she could be let in. Beryl did hand milking here as the farmer only kept cows for the family use, for their milk, cream and butter. Beryl says "Believe me you have never tasted butter like it". Whilst at the farm she picked fruit, dug up potatoes, hoed and weeded. At the farm they held shooting parties for gentlemen, Lord Leigh of Stoneleigh Abbey was often a guest as were the Cockburn's of the port family.

As Beryl was only seventeen she was allowed out until 10 pm, unless there was something special on and then it was extended. She met a local farmer's son at the Young Farmers Club who happened to have a car, so her social life changed. Two Land Girls who lived in one of the cottages further up the road from the farm introduced her to the local pub The Crab Mill Inn, it was here that she met her future husband, Eric, who was on leave from the Navy. At the time she did not know that one of the locals had bet him that he would not walk her back to the farm (they lost). When he returned to Portsmouth after his leave they wrote to each other and met each time he came home.

She had been working on the farm for eighteen months when she started to get itchy feet and decided to transfer to a hostel in Greatheed Road, Leamington Spa. The Land Girls went to work in various villages doing all kinds of work. One of the jobs she remembers well was at Warwick Castle, weeding carrots, they were about six inches high and the weeds were twelve inches. They worked there for weeks, although they did not mind, as it was a beautiful setting alongside the River Avon.

Following the removal of her appendix, Beryl did light duties at Whitehill, a former bomber station, just outside Stratford Upon Avon, which the WLA took over when the military moved out. At Whitehill the girls were collected by the Army and taken to the camp at Long Marston for dances, this also happened with the RAF when they were taken to Fairford in Gloucestershire.

When she was fit she moved to Fell Mill Farm, Shipston on Stour, to work for the farmer Fred Bryan. Here she took up her milking skills again and worked alongside Jack Holtem, who was the head cow man. She got to know his family well and has remained friends ever since. Beryl said this was a wonderful time. She and the girls had cheese and beetroot sandwiches day after day, until they were sick of them, and she did not always eat hers, but Jack's brother Ken would take extra cake which his mother had baked and he always gave her half, it tasted like heaven. She thinks he was sweet on her, as he always wanted to take her out, but things were getting serious with Eric, although she did sometimes go to the local pub with him for a drink.

One day as she was milking, a man from "Warag" (this was a department set up during the war to monitor food production) called at the farm and said he wanted to get her into relief work for the whole of Warwickshire. This involved being ready at a moments notice to go anywhere in Warwickshire, perhaps for a week or two, if someone was ill and unable to do the milking. In spite of the fact that she did not want to do this kind of work and neither did her boss want her to go, she was sent for a trial. Yes, Beryl did work all over Warwickshire and some farmers never even gave her a drink. Then one day whilst working for a family, she thought enough is enough, she was tired of living out of a suitcase, so she told the people that she wanted to return to Fred Bryan's farm, which she did and worked there until she was married.

She served in the WLA for three years and really enjoyed the life, particularly the countryside. After all these years she still has contact with the girls she worked with at Shipston on Stour.

When Beryl and Eric got married they went to live in a cottage, which belonged to Mr Saunders. She had turned a full circle returning to where she began in the WLA. She worked with her husband on the land pea and potato picking, hoeing, mangol chopping and threshing which is a dirty job. When she had her three boys she still worked on the land, which must have been very hard to cope with everything.

Her three boys all went to Moreton Morrell Agricultural College where they gained top honours.

Beryl and Eric still enjoy going into the countryside, they presently live at Galley Common, Nr. Nuneaton. She said that when they first moved there it was like being in the countryside, but now houses surround them.

Thank you to Beryl for her story.

~~~~~~~~~~~~~~~~~~~~~~~~~~~~~

Joan McNally nee Haselock.

Joan was born in Coventry and Warwickshire Hospital on the 15th November 1924. Her parents had a small provisions shop in Primrose Hill Street, Coventry. When she was seven years old the family moved to Ferndale Road, Binley Woods.

Joan worked at the General Electric Company at Stoke, Coventry as a clerk/typist from 1939 to 1942. She decided she would like to join the Timber Corps, but was told that Warwickshire needed Land Girls. She was 17 at this time too young for the other services with a minimum age at entry of 18. Joan joined The Women's Land Army early in 1943. She was sent to Coombe Abbey Farm where she was employed doing general farm and land work, but disliked milking the cows and using the big farm horses, for which she was given no training. Joan was pleased to be transferred to the Wyken Industrial Hostel, for displaced persons during the Second World War. It is believed that this was situated on land where Walsgrave Hospital is now. There were other such hostels in and around Coventry, such as The Chase Industrial Hostel, Willenhall, Finham Park Industrial Hostel, Keresley Hostel, Baginton Fields and Whoberley. These hostels were for persons (mainly males) from all over

Britain and Ireland to stay in, after being redirected by the Government to work in Coventry, building pre-fabs etc., or working in the factories on war work These hostels were nothing to do with the WLA.

Joan was the only Land Girl to live at the hostel, she was joined later by two other Land Army girls, but they lived at their own homes.

She was paid £2.8.0s (£2.40) per week, with her uniform supplied free. She and the two other girls grew vegetables for consumption by the residents of the hostels. She used the facilities of the hostel such as table tennis and played chess with some of the displaced persons, many of whom were foreign and did not speak English. There was also a dance hall at the hostel.

Joan says that the experience of being in the WLA has not had any effect on her life, as she has always loved the land, gardening and the changing seasons.

As with other Land Army girls she received a letter from The Queen Mother in appreciation of her loyal and devoted service, which lasted from 29th March 1943 until 23rd May 1946.

Joan still possesses a Warwickshire News Sheet dated September 1943 in which she had a poem printed, although she does not remember submitting this. The poem is as follows:-

Sacrifice.

1. Oh! Dear! Sighed the wheat,
   Life so far has been sweet,
   But I fear its my doom,
   To die very soon.

2. The Harvest is here,
   And to me it is clear,
   I can no longer sleep,
   For the reaper must reap.

3. I'll try not to trouble,
   Very soon I'll be stubble,
   Tho' I weep, tho' I sigh,
   'Tis best I should die.

4. There's a war on, and so,
   I am needed I know,
   Here take thou my head,
   For my country needs BREAD.

J.HASELOCK 115671

When she was demobbed she stayed on at the hostel and worked as a receptionist/typist.

Joan currently lives in West Sussex with her husband of 56 years.

Medicine in the Home in the first half of the Twentieth Century.

Before the National Health Act was passed in 1946, the provision of health care had to be paid for. The better off could afford the charge of around sixpence a visit to the doctor, or to call him out when someone in the family was ill. The poor had the option of joining a scheme such as that provided by the General Dispensary or Provident Dispensary, which provided cover for the family at a charge of one penny a week. Even this small cost was beyond the means of the poorest in the community. The National Insurance Act of 1911 provided health cover for the head of the household in work and contributing to the scheme, but did not cover members of his family. This left many people with no provision at all should they fall ill.

Healthcare was usually left in the hands of the women in the family, either the mother or grandmother. They carried out the nursing in the home, frequently with the help of neighbours. If a family was too poor to pay for medical cover they were probably inadequately fed. Poor nutrition made people vulnerable to infection and liable to such conditions as rickets, stunted growth and weakness, especially children. Immunisation against such diseases as smallpox was provided free of charge from the nineteenth century and diphtheria by 1930, although not everyone took advantage of its availability.

Children were the most vulnerable members of society and a high percentage died before the age of five. The greatest killer of very young children was diarrhoea, due to poor hygiene. Breast-fed babies were far less vulnerable to infection, but many poor women had to work and their babies were weaned on to a bottle, or they were so undernourished themselves that their milk soon dried up. Whatever the reason for bottle-feeding a baby, they were liable to pick up infection from the teats and bottles, which were not sterilized. Teats were often no more than a rag squeezed into the neck of a bottle.

Childhood illnesses such as mumps, measles and whooping cough were far more severe at the beginning of the century and children frequently died in an epidemic. More severe illnesses like diphtheria and scarlet fever were the cause of many deaths. Isolation of the patient was advised and treatment by a physician, but in the poorest, most overcrowded homes it was impossible to set aside a bedroom for the infected person. In the case of scarlet fever it became common for the patient to be taken to an isolation hospital. When Beatrice Callow went down with scarlet fever in the early part of the twentieth century, arrangements were made for an ambulance to take her to the isolation hospital. She had to wait three hours for it to arrive. Her family were not allowed to visit because of infection, but her mother and sister went every day to read the bulletin board outside the hospital. Notices were posted up every day to inform relatives of the condition of the patients inside. When her mother saw 'Very poorly indeed' written against her daughter's name, she cried all the way home. While confined to bed the child needed to use the toilet, but could not attract the attention of the nurse and eventually wet the bed. When the nurse discovered the wet bed she was very angry and smacked the poor child across the face. All the children, despite their illness were dosed with a laxative called 'Black Jack' on a Friday night. Beatrice spent seven weeks in hospital and ten weeks away from school.

Dorothy Parker caught scarlet fever at the age of fifteen in 1928 and initially she was kept at home with a disinfected sheet across the bedroom door. Later she was taken to Gulson Road Hospital where she was kept in isolation for six weeks. All her clothes were burnt, even a brand new pair of shoes. Even in the late 1940s treatment had changed very little. John Hockton caught the disease around 1948 and was isolated in a bedroom at home. A sheet soaked in disinfectant was stretched across the doorway, as he remained confined to his room being nursed by his mother for many weeks under the care of a doctor. Like Dorothy, his clothes were destroyed and his books and room were sprayed with disinfectant.

Diphtheria killed a great many children in the early years of the twentieth century. Beatrice Callow wrote graphically of the treatment she received at the beginning of the century* when the doctor treated the family with contempt because they lived in great poverty in a court dwelling off Much Park Street. She describes how her mother had to pawn the bedclothes to pay for the medicine to paint her throat. She recovered, but a neighbour's son was not so fortunate. Her care was wholly in the hands of her mother and the kind neighbours in the court and a sympathetic district nurse. There was no isolation in this situation, but fortunately her younger sister did not catch the disease.

In 1931 when Megan Saxelby was eleven years old, she developed a sore throat and fever. Not until the following day did her mother realise how ill she was and sent for a doctor. By this time her throat was very inflamed and a grey membrane had grown across her throat and she was delirious. The doctor diagnosed diphtheria and a neighbour volunteered to go to the hospital to collect the serum. The doctor returned to administer the serum to combat the disease. The syringe appeared to be about six inches long with a needle of the same length, which terrified his poor nervous patient. As she was extremely thin, the doctor had some difficulty in finding a suitable site for the injection. She was nursed at home by her mother, as there were no other children in the family. The usual precaution of stretching a sheet across the doorway soaked in carbolic, was practiced, but it is doubtful whether this served much purpose in this case.

Over the following weeks as she improved, the doctor came to take swabs of her throat to send for analysis. Three clear swabs were required before she was allowed to return to school. Weeks went by and the infection was still present. Eventually she went back to school, but a day later the district nurse came to remove her from the classroom and sent her home again as she was still carrying the disease in her throat. The district nurse recommended the child's mother to paint her throat with Mandel's Paint, a thick, treacly substance, which was administered with a brush. Even after more than seventy years she remembers that it tasted like cat's urine; presumably it smelled like that. It was three months before she was allowed back to school, by which time she had missed so much of her school work, she never really caught up with the others.

Tonsils were often a source of infection and the general consensus in the medical profession was that if they caused trouble they should come out. Beatrice Callow had a terrible experience when her tonsils were removed in Coventry & Warwickshire Hospital around 1908, following repeated bouts of tonsillitis. She and her mother arrived for the first consultation at 1.45pm in plenty of time for her 2pm appointment. The waiting room was already crowded, but no doctors arrived for an hour, when five or six doctors dressed in white coats strode into the department to complete silence. Within minutes there was great activity amongst the nurses, but it was 5.30pm before Beatrice was called in.

There was no thought to reassuring the children, no kindness or understanding from the medical staff. Only one person showed any sympathy or tried to make the children smile, and he was the porter, Charlie. When Beatrice finally saw the doctor he had a lamp strapped to his head and reminded her of a butcher. Both the child and her mother were frightened when he bawled out 'Open your mouth.' He called for his students to come and take a look at her throat. As she closed her mouth to swallow he shouted at her and she began to cry. He pushed her away and told them to return the following week for removal of the tonsils and adenoids.

When they arrived to keep that appointment they were shown into a smaller waiting room filled with children and their mothers sitting on wooden benches. An hour went by before Charlie came to fetch the child. He was kind and reassuring as he took her to the operating theatre and lifted her on to the operating table. A mask was clamped over her mouth and she heard the surgeon say 'Ready.' Before she could protest she lost consciousness. When she came round she was lying on a rubber sheet on the floor with many other children all crying for their mothers. The sheet was covered in blood, which must have been a terrifying sight for these children. A nurse came in and clapped her hands together, shouting, 'Stop this noise at once all of you, or none of you will go home at all.' She made them get up and stand in file, still bleeding, and walk to the waiting room. The nurse sponged their faces and allowed them to join their mothers. They were told to return in two weeks.

At the sight of her daughter, Beatrice's mother burst into tears. She had to carry her ten-year old daughter, still groggy from the anaesthetic and loss of blood, from Stoney Stanton Road to Vecqueray Street, with only a short tram journey in the middle. There were no ambulances to take the patients home, it was up to them to find a means of getting back. She spent another two weeks confined to bed before returning to the hospital for a check-up.

Megan Saxelby had a pleasanter experience of having her tonsils removed in 1923. Then only two and a half years old, her mother arranged for her to have her tonsils out at home. The kitchen table had to be scrubbed and disinfected before the doctor and district nurse carried out the operation. Her parents were better off than Beatrice Callow's family, although they only lived in a modest house in Thomas Street and were far from well off. They paid one shilling a week to be on a local doctor's panel, although the operation had to be paid for separately.

Many people belonged to the Hospital Saturday Fund, which covered the cost of hospitalisation, ambulances and convalescence. The council also ran convalescent homes at Allesley Hall and The Towers, in Kenilworth. Hospitals were paid for by charitable donations and money collected during the carnival procession, which always stopped outside Coventry & Warwickshire Hospital, to the delight of the patients and nursing staff. Patients in their beds were wheeled out to watch the floats go by.

Hospital was not a place that people wanted to enter, as it was rumoured that once inside you were unlikely to come out again. Admittedly those who went in with terminal illness were unlikely to recover, but operations were becoming more successful by the twentieth century and isolation was the greatest safeguard against the spread of contagious diseases before the development of a more comprehensive inoculation programme. However, hospital was a place of dread for many people and home remedies were very popular for working and middle class families all over the country.

Chemist shops produced their own patent medicines to treat common illnesses such as colds, skin complaints, weakness, etc. Local pharmacists such as Bird's in Spon Street and Welton's in Bishop Street advertised their own special brand of tonic, cough mixture or pills for a variety of complaints. Some of the more enterprising concerns began advertising nationally, advocating the wonders of their tonic wine, pills or ointment. In those days a company could claim that a product would cure an enormous range of problems from backache to piles, a practice that is no longer allowed. On the 1st October 1917 the Midland Daily Telegraph ran an advertisement for Clarke's Blood Mixture, priced 2s 9d per bottle, claiming it cured 'Open wounds from knee to foot.' Bad legs, abcesses, ulcers, glandular swellings, piles, eczema, boils, pimples and eruptions, rheumatism and kindred complaints were all said to be cured by the wonder mixture.

During the First World War many of the advertisements held the message that it would benefit the product's users at a time of stress and upheaval. One such was Clymol, a special food recommended for disability, convalescent patients, etc., priced at 2s 6d for 1lb. A few ounces a week was enough to put on weight, they claimed, 'A wonderful wartime standby.' These advertisements frequently held a recommendation by a satisfied user endorsing the claims. Many were aimed at the munitions girls who now had disposable income to lavish on face and hand creams. Icilma Cream, 'For the girl behind the gun,' with an accompanying picture of a munitions worker, urged girls to use their face cream night and morning for a good complexion at a cost 1s per pot. Beecham's Pills, a name equally well known to post Second World War generations were advertising in 1917 that their digestive and restorative medicine would give people the good health to 'Do their bit,' for the war effort

Health care was a business, promoted to its customers in the same way as any other commodity. Frequently advertisements appeared for trusses and other surgical appliances to ease problems such as hernias that were not routinely cured by surgery. In 1917 an advertisement ran in The Midland Daily Telegraph for a Mr. Matthew Bennett, Bonesetter, of Emscote Lodge, Warwick. He would hold a surgery at the White Lion Hotel, Smithford Street, Coventry, every Friday from 2-4pm to set broken bones, or could be contacted at his home in the mornings and evenings. It seems unimaginable to those brought up with the National Health Service that anyone could make a living in this way. It does not say that he was a doctor or qualified in any way for this occupation. Dorothy, born in 1913, broke her arm when a child, but was taken to her own doctor to be fitted with heavy wooden splints, which remained in place until it healed.

After the First World War these advertisements increased in number with no brake upon the claims they made. The Coventry Standard of the 9th April 1920 ran an advert for Phosferine Tonic medicine. It was one of those cure-all medicines that claimed to treat chronic neuralgia, malaria, shock, influenza, insomnia, and nerve problems. The range of illness was so wide that it was incredible that readers were gullible enough to believe it. De Witt's advertised it's medication as 'Pink pills for pale people.' Towle's Pills professed to be 'The finest remedy in the world,' women's unfailing friend. Too reserved to say they were for period pains, but the implication was there. Many adverts carried pictures of smiling children helped to good health by such nutritious foods as Bird's Custard.

Cures for colds were some of the more prolific forms of advertising. We know that there is still no cure for the common cold, but people believed the claims of these drug companies, when in fact they could only relieve the symptoms. In 1920 Scott's Cough Linctus was advertised in the Coventry Standard at 1s 3d and 3s per bottle, with another called Peps for coughs and cold appearing in the same edition, while Quimphos for coughs and influenza, 3s from chemists can be seen in an edition of 1921. Another was 'Venos Lightening Cough Cure.' There must have been hundreds of companies making such claims on a regular basis. These adverts held the stamp of authority to encourage the public to buy them.

Some patent medicines were positively harmful to the patient, as in the case of some teething powders for babies, which contained harmful mercury, causing a complaint called Pink disease. Tonics often contained laudanum or alcohol to which the patient became addicted. There was no body in place to oversee the safety of medicines as there is now, although of course it was not in the interest of any manufacturer to produce something that would make its potential customers ill.

One of the most common forms of medicine in use was laxatives. Even in the twentieth century the old treatment of brimstone and treacle or liquorice powder was practiced as a purge at the end of each week. There was an obsession (and still is in some people) with making sure the bowels were open every day. Diet was often poor and inadequate and shared toilets in a court dwelling or multi-occupied houses must have been inconvenient at times, which could contribute to the problem of constipation. However, the widespread use of laxatives from an early age only escalated the problem in later life. Manufactures of patent medicines were quick to stress the efficacy of their products to an audience only too eager to make purges more palatable. The makers of California Syrup of Figs were recommending their medicine in 1917 for babies and children; when the tongue was coated and the throat sore; even when a person had diarrhoea! In 1920 Hartley's Three Salts included constipation in a list of ailments such as rheumatism, gout, stomach problems, liver and kidneys, which would all benefit from a dose of their medicine. As J.A.C. Brown wrote in the Pears Medical Encyclopaedia, published in 1962 'One cannot die of constipation but one can become very ill with pills designed to treat it.'

For a few pence remedies could be bought from the local huckster's shop, where manufacturers such as Stotherts carded a variety medicines, although even these were beyond the means of the poorer members of society and they made do with homemade treatments. Coughs and colds were helped by boiling the zest of a lemon in water and sweetening with sugar or honey. Camomile tea was used to help kidneys, rather than buying one of the many brands of kidney and liver pills available. To relieve the symptoms of bronchitis and chesty coughs camphorated oil might be warmed and rubbed on to the chest and back, or a linseed poultice strapped to the chest. If all of these proved too expensive then goose grease might be the last resort. Croup associated with bad chests and breathing difficulties in children was treated with bread poultices or steam kettles. Raspberry vinegar was used to relieve period pains and aspirin was cheaply available for the treatment of pain of any kind. If a person suffered from indigestion and milk did not neutralise the acid in the stomach then remedies such as Setlitz Powders could be taken mixed with water.

Children frequently suffered from sore eyes and earache. Borasic crystals dissolved in water bathed on the eyes or golden eye ointment helped to relieve the symptoms, but if that was beyond your means cold tea was very effective. Earache was relieved by pouring warmed olive oil into the ear, however, this was no solution to middle ear infection, which could be very serious and result in impaired hearing. Childhood infections like chickenpox, mumps and German measles were considered fairly mild illnesses by the mid 1940s. It was not uncommon for mothers to ask if their children could play with the afflicted patient in the hope of getting the illness over with while young. The only treatment for the itchy rash associated with them was Calomine lotion. Impetigo, a highly infectious skin disease, usually on the face was treated with gentian violet. This antiseptic could also be used on throat sores and those associated with chickenpox in the throat.

The skin could become chapped and sore in cold weather or due to a job where the hands were constantly in water. There were plenty of proprietary brands of ointment available, but one of the cheapest was Melrose wax or even paraffin wax on which it was based. Oil of cloves was used to treat chilblains, a very common complaint before the widespread use of central heating, which caused agony to the sufferers, but a free alternative was to immerse the affected toes in urine. Warts were said to be cured by rubbing a wet match head over them. Many people suffered from stiff joints, rheumatism and muscle pain. Again there were plenty of remedies on the market claiming to relieve the symptoms, but for those who could not afford such medicines there was a massage with embrocation ointment or wintergreen, or even horse liniment if that was all that was available.

Dorothy's mother, Mabel Christen, always advocated that good health was as catching as bad health. She did not believe in pampering her children or dressing them in too many clothes. Fresh air was good for them and she encouraged them to spend as much time as possible out of doors. The environment in which people lived certainly influenced their state of health. Those who had a better diet and lived in a less polluted atmosphere had a greater chance of survival. The better off, however, were not immune to infectious diseases, but they had a higher life expectancy, as they still do. We have a lot to be grateful for since the advent of the National Health Service.

Thank you to all those who provided me with information.

* See Hurdy Gurdy Days, one of our previous publications.

~~~~~~~~~~~~~~~~~~~~~~~~~~~

Betty Jones.

When Betty was born in April 1920 in a house called Bramble Cottage, in Bournemouth, she was not aware that it had been named after Bramble Street, in Coventry, where her parents' first home had been situated and where her older brothers had been born. Her family name was Hattrell, a well-known Coventry family. Her connections with Coventry were strong, not only because of family ties, but it was to play an important part in her future. Her first experience of the city came when visiting her relatives during her childhood and the deep impression that stayed in her memory was of the poverty of the children she saw on attending Sunday school there.

When she left school at the age of fourteen she was drawn towards a career in nursing, for she never forgot those poor children and adults in Coventry and wanted to help them. However, her father seemed very reluctant to let his daughter enter the nursing profession and persuaded her to find a job in an office instead. She worked in the office of a builders' merchant in Bournemouth, but constantly thought of becoming a nurse. Whenever she voiced her ambition her father gave her no encouragement, although she never understood why he was so reluctant. Maybe he thought she would be exposed to sights and be required to perform duties he found distasteful.

After five years of office work she took matters into her own hands and applied to work in the offices of Bourne and Hollingsworth in London, with the object of investigating the possibility of being taken on for training at a London hospital. National events took a hand in her plans, however, when six months after arriving in London war broke out and the company felt they could not be responsible for their young women employees and sent them back home. Bourne and Hollingsworth had connections with Beales department store in Bournemouth and Betty was transferred to their offices, away from the possible bombing of London.

Back in her home town again and still longing to be a nurse, she volunteered to become a VAD with the Red Cross. As she did not object to moving away from Bournemouth, she was sent to an army barracks at Didcot in Oxfordshire, where preparations were being made to deal with health problems caused by the war. It was not the kind of nursing she had expected and she soon became restless. She decided to write to the Victoria Hospital in Swindon (now known as the Princess Margaret Hospital) to see if they were willing to take her on as a trainee nurse, and she was given an interview. Her actions were treated with suspicion by the army authorities and led to many questions being asked, for they were very conscious of security at the barracks and wondered why she was planning to leave them so soon.

At the interview she met a woman almoner, a position that no longer exists, who performed the important function of liasing with patients, their families and the hospital, a type of welfare officer. She looked after Betty while she was in Swindon for the interview. Betty felt sure that she would be offered a place, especially as she was measured for a uniform following the interview. The dress of stiff, mauve and white striped material had to be a regulation two inches above the ankle. She left Swindon full of optimism for the future; it was 1940, she was twenty years old and she had just been offered the opportunity to do the thing she had always wanted to do.

Back at Didcot camp she had to undergo yet more questioning, but eventually she was allowed to take up her place at Swindon. Arriving by train, she was met by the Home Sister who was in charge of the nurses' home. Betty's first question to the Sister was whether her bicycle, which was sent in advance, had arrived. Assured that it had, she accompanied the Sister to the nurses' home. The Victorian hospital, with more recent additions was situated in the new town of Swindon, the old town being based around the GWR works. The hospital is now wholly concerned with geriatric care, but in 1940 it was the general hospital.

Betty's first day on the medical ward was a baptism of fire, when the Sister ordered her to assist a nurse behind some screens. She was confronted by a scene she had not anticipated; a naked, dead man was being laid out before being taken to the mortuary. Not only had she never seen a dead body before, she had never seen a naked man either. Recovering from the shock she was of little help to the nurse, who seemed very annoyed by her presence and sent her away. She learned later that the nurse was angry with the Sister for sending such an inexperienced girl, rather than angry with Betty. This was Nurse Rummings, a few years Betty's senior, who became one of her best friends.

Training was a matter of learning on the job, watching and copying senior nurses. There were endless cleaning jobs to be done despite the services of a ward maid. There was never a minute to spare, for if all regular tasks had been completed there was an extra work book containing additional jobs, such as scrape the fluff off the wheels of the beds, pull the beds away from the walls and clean behind and high dusting. Another extra job was filling the autoclaver ready for sterilization. Dressings of all kinds did not come sealed and ready for use as they do today, the nurse had to line the metal container with strips of linen, squares of gauze and hand-made cotton wool balls until it was full. It was taken away to be autoclaved (sterilized by heating). When returned the contents were dark brown from the heating process. Lectures had to be attended straight from a shift on the wards. Many a nurse fell asleep during the lecture, huddled in her long, navy blue cloak, tired out from a long night shift. Study had to be done in their spare time. The newest trainees slept in long dormitories, so finding a quiet place to study could be a problem. The more senior trainees had their own room and Betty was lucky that her friend Nurse Rummings allowed her to use her room to study in peace. All nurses had to keep their sleeping area or room clean and tidy.

Very shortly after Betty began her training, she was moved to night duty and used as a runner. This involved moving from one ward to another assisting the nurse in charge of thirty patients. Wards were long rooms with a centrally placed desk for the nurse. One of the jobs Betty hated most was being sent to the kitchens to fill the large cans with milk for each ward. When the light was switched on in the kitchen she saw that the floor was covered in cockroaches. She had to steel herself to walk across the floor as the insects scuttled away out of sight; it happened every night but she always found it very unpleasant. Knowing how tired Betty was on the night shift, Nurse

Rummings encouraged her to have a rest in the office if it was quiet, but would kick the door to warn her of the approach of Sister. Betty soon became known as Hatty to the other nurses, due to her surname Hattrell.

Sisters had a great deal of power and the Matron was supreme. Nursing was a female profession, whereas doctors were exclusively male in Betty's experience and rather aloof. The hospital system was very hierarchical, with trainee nurses at the bottom. There was no privacy for the patients, only screens, which had to be carried from the end of the ward. They were not the more modern wheeled variety, but heavy wooden frames with curtained panels. A nurse was not allowed to run except in the case of fire or haemorrhage and never if she was carrying screens.

Over the five years of her training Betty covered every aspect of nursing, surgical, general, theatre work, terminal cases and children's wards. Of all the patients she helped to nurse over that time, the one that affected her most of all was the case of a young child called David, who was rushed in with appendicitis. He was a farmer's son, who was in the habit of eating grass and this may have been a contributing factor in his illness. Following emergency surgery he remained desperately ill and died soon afterwards. This was before the widespread use of penicillin and it made Betty feel so helpless in the face of a severe infection.

The war did not affect Swindon to any great extent, although a ward was earmarked for war casualties. RAF Lynham was situated fairly close to Swindon and suffered one severe raid, which brought an influx of casualties to the hospital. Despite all the hard work there were lighter moments, such as the time when a down-and-out was brought in. He allowed himself to be cleaned up, but would not remove a filthy cap from his head. When Betty noticed it was moving of its own volition the nurses forced him into the sluice to remove it. The handyman, Sid, was called to dispose of the verminous object. During the short hours of leisure time the nurses managed to get away from the hospital environment, Betty made full use of her bicycle that had caused her so much concern on arrival in Swindon. She and her friends cycled into the surrounding countryside to enjoy the freedom and fresh air.

In 1945 Betty took her final examination and qualified as a state registered nurse. The war in Europe was at an end when she heard the results on the 8th June. She decided to move on and applied to become a district nurse in Coventry. After initial training in Rochdale, she began her life as a Queen's nurse in Coventry. The service was based at a large house in Park Road, which is now Cheshunt School. The nurses lived in houses nearby, but reported to headquarters every morning to be given their duties for the day. It was an independent service, not attached to a particular surgery, but available to any doctor in the city. Only the senior nurse had the use of a car, all the other nurses used bicycles to reach their patients. Betty eventually became senior nurse and took driving instruction from another nurse.

Betty, who had wanted to work with poor people, was initially assigned to Kenilworth Road, the most affluent part of the city, although eventually she did nurse the poor. When the nurses had completed their duties they returned to headquarters to report on the progress of patients and what was required for further visits. Some of the most deprived areas she worked in were those around Windsor Street, with some of the worst slum housing in the city. The court dwellings were small and jerry-built, but the people made up for their inadequate surroundings by the care they lavished on their sick relatives and neighbours. Anything that was required was found somehow, despite their poverty.

Sometimes two nurses went on the rounds together if there was a lot of heavy lifting to do. Betty remembers having to lift a patient with a double hip plaster, standing at the head of the bed and hauling the patient up the bed. Often a member of the family would assist in the process. District nurses treated an enormous variety of complaints in the patient's own home. Bedsores were a common affliction when a person was bedridden for a long time. They were treated twice a day when they became a serious problem. The patient's family was trained to dress them too, for this helped to ease the burden on the nurse. Prevention was better than cure and nurses did all in their power to stop them occurring. At each visit they rubbed the patient's back and pressure points with caster oil and zinc, massaging the areas and washing afterwards. Immediately a sore was noticed action was taken to prevent its spread. Bedsores were considered a poor reflection on a nurse's skill, but the fact was that patients spent too long confined to bed. The nurses used certain devices to relieve the pressure; rubber, air-filled rings to reduce pressure on hips and buttocks and heel rings made of cotton wool, as that was such a vulnerable place. The idea of getting people up and moving about as quickly as possible has done more to combat bedsores than all the devices used to relieve the condition.

Ulcers, especially varicose ulcers were another condition that the nurses treated. They tried many remedies, but it was a matter of trial and error. Betty once tried soaking strips of linen in cod liver oil and laying them over the ulcer. The most common ailments were chest conditions associated with poor air quality, strong tobacco and poor working conditions, such as coalmines and dusty environments. A steam kettle and friars balsam was the usual treatment for breathing problems associated with bronchitis and asthma.

Not all patients went into hospital for operations, some doctors still performed minor operations on the kitchen table, especially in cases of tonsillectomy. Betty assisted Dr. Beryl in many operations to remove tonsils and other surgical procedures. They always asked the family of the patient to provide three things in preparation for the operation; a bucket, a bowl and a newspaper, and if possible a clean towel too. The newspaper went on the floor, the bucket was placed on top to receive soiled dressings and the bowl was for washing. The nurse boiled the instruments in a saucepan, scrubbed the table and sterilized the dressings by placing them in a biscuit tin and baking them in the oven, in exactly the same way as the autoclaver did in hospital. Daily visits were made to the patient afterwards until they recovered.

They treated many terminally ill patients in their own home, in addition to those who had undergone unsuccessful surgical operations and were sent home to die. Others suffered from oedema, where the body fills with fluid due to kidney failure, heart failure or some other complaint. As they could not move about easily, they eventually became bedridden and in need of constant care. There were very few T.B. patients treated in the home by the late 1940s, as effective drugs were available to treat patients and sanatoria were common. Betty never came into contact with any cases when on the district.

The arsenal of drugs in the hands of the nursing profession was very limited even in the 1940s. They relied on good hygiene and devoted care in a great many cases. Kaolin poultices were widely and effectively used for drawing out infection from wounds. Antibiotics were just coming into use when Betty began work in Coventry, but only used sparingly. Penicillin did not come in convenient ampoules, but in tablet form, which had to be dissolved in a measured amount of water and drawn into a syringe before being injected into a patient.

Within a month of her arrival in Coventry to take up her post as a Queen's nurse, Betty met her future husband, Gil. She left nursing when she was expecting her first child, but returned when her son went to boarding school early in the 1960s. She began work at the clinic in Barker's Butts Lane, in Coundon. There she weighed the babies, advised the mothers on child care and assisted the Health Visitors in their work. Another aspect of her work was carried out in schools as a nit nurse, checking children's heads for lice. She often had to administer the special shampoo to kill the lice if parents would not co-operate. She found her work in the clinic and school very enjoyable and it fitted in with her family commitments. She finally retired from nursing in 1968 after a very fulfilling career. She never regretted her decision to come to Coventry and it has become her home for the past fifty-seven years.

Interviewed July 2002.

Coventry Stroke Group.

Coventry Stroke Group was started in 1977, initiated by a Speech Therapist, who asked a couple of stroke patients what they thought about forming a group to include them and their partners. The group was formed and initially they held meetings at Faseman House, Tile Hill, Coventry. The group then moved to The Stone House, in Allesley village, Coventry. This was a lovely old building in which to hold the meetings, but was totally impractical, due to the steps and small passageways. We then moved to the Wilfred Spencer Centre in Allesley Park, one of the first groups to meet there. We still meet at this centre every other Monday evening.

My father had a serious stroke at the age of sixty years and went on to live until he was seventy-three although, at that time, help and support was non-existent. He always said that when he passed away he did not want any floral tributes, but I wanted to mark his death in some way that would benefit people like him. My involvement with the group began when my father died in 1981 and I took a donation to The Stone House and somehow got roped in as a volunteer, then as Treasurer and now Chairman for a number of years. At that time there was an article in the Coventry Evening Telegraph, stating that the Stroke Group had just acquired a "Splink" Machine (this is similar to a computer, but buttons could be pressed to phrase certain questions and answers). The only drawback was it had to be used in one person's house at a time, which meant some members had to wait a long time for its use and some people could not cope with it. I think the reason for this is that it confused them, particularly if they had not previously used a computer. Speech therapy is no longer provided, as it became obvious that stroke sufferers are too tired to concentrate in the evenings and apart from this it did divide the group into two parts.

The group is very lively and we have all kinds of activities. We try to stimulate their minds in every way possible. One of the events we have each year is a Strawberry Tea (although it is held in the evening), at the Centre and is enjoyed by all. Annually we used to have a Skittles Match and Buffet, which was held in the evening at The Jaguar Sports and Social Club, but now we go at lunchtime to The Cuttle Inn at Long Itchington. We have a pre-booked buffet and then a game of skittles, the members really like this outing. The reason we have changed from the Jaguar is that by going at lunchtime a ride through the countryside is appreciated.

Also in the autumn we have a Fish and Chip Supper, which we order from the chip shop opposite the Centre, in addition we manage to fit in a Sausage and Chip Supper. The committee usually prepare a Ploughman's Supper and a Cheese and Wine Evening during the year, as food is something they can still enjoy even if they cannot pursue more active events. A number of different quizzes are held, one is an Advert Quiz, where the members have to guess the name of the manufacturer or the name of the product. We also have "Who wants to be a millionaire"; this is carried out in teams and adapted to suit the group. The writer has also recorded some music and we have Name that Tune, which is enjoyed by all.

At Christmas time we do a Christmas Quiz (done on a Christmas theme) and Christmas Anagrams, which the members take home and bring back after the recess. If they are correct they get a prize (I think that their families probably help with this). We always go out for a Christmas Lunch, although it is quite hard to find a suitable venue as we have to be aware of steps or stairs and must be accessible for disabled. We also have a Christmas Party at the Centre for which we cater ourselves. Some time ago we asked the members to bring along some food and ended up with so many boxes of Mr. Kipling's Mince Pies, it was a good job that committee members did a selection of sandwiches and nibbles. The next time we suggested to them what food they could bring, and this worked out fine. One year we had outside caterers, but we decided that the committee would do the catering in future, the reason being that it turned out to be too expensive.

A few years ago the staff of Marks and Spencer, Coventry, donated a large screen television and video recorder to the group, this was always a hit with the men if it was showing foot-ball and England were playing. They had beer and sandwiches and they did get a bit loud urging them on. Every year we have a Tombola, we hold raffles at every meeting and also have a Sales Table, for which members bring articles to sell, with the proceeds going towards our funds.

Recently, we were able to donate one thousand pounds to the Stroke Unit at Walsgrave Hospital, Coventry, and wheelchairs and patient boards were purchased for over the beds, which give details of their progress and activities. Coventry should have had a specialised Stroke Unit long ago, as other areas had, this one was only opened about three years ago. The writer has visited the unit on occasions and been very impressed. It consists of an eight-bedded ward with a dedicated team of nurses, speech therapists and occupational therapists. In my opinion it is beneficial as the same team look after the same patients and therefore do see what progress is being made. There can be nothing worse for a stroke sufferer to be in a general ward where patients who have been admitted after them are discharged before them. In a general ward they do not seem to get the physiotherapy or attention they receive in the Stroke Unit. Members of our group have said that there should be more beds, but I feel if the unit gets bigger then perhaps the staff would not be able to cope. However, should extra staff be taken on to cover extra beds it could be successful and more beds are definitely needed.

Our group does encourage the stroke sufferer's partner to come to the meetings, as it is good for them to have a break as well. Some people who have strokes can have a change of personality, this is understandable and must be very frustrating, particularly if you have been an active person and then have to rely on others to help you. The worst scenario is when the person cannot speak, they try to communicate but nothing makes sense; no wonder they get bad tempered and nasty. It is not very nice for their partner, even though they do not mean it, it is still hurtful. The writer has noticed that some of the members cannot deal with money and are vulnerable to exploitation. Some cannot read because their sight has been affected by the stroke. Lack of concentration also seems to be prevalent, so that is why we have quizzes etc. to encourage these people.

A stroke strikes without warning and is the third most common disease after heart failure and cancer. A stroke means the sudden destruction of part of the brain by a haemorrhage into the brain, or by blocking a blood vessel which supplies the brain. If the haemorrhage is large the patient normally goes straight into a coma and possibly dies in a matter of hours or days.

The brain controls movement, feeling, language, thought and emotion. Damage to any area of the brain causes disturbance of one or more of these functions. In some people their face becomes twisted, an arm hangs, the leg weak and stiff. Some people have difficulty in swallowing and have to have their food liquidised. Each time a person visits their doctor they should ask to have their blood pressure checked as this could help prevent a stroke.

When a person initially has a stroke and cannot speak properly or be understood they should really have speech therapy straight away. As mentioned previously, this is where a dedicated Stroke Unit comes into its own. Also family and friends can help by speaking slowly and clearly. It is important to listen attentively to the patient's speech, even if it is difficult to understand. It is useful to encourage the patient to use hand signals, writing or drawing to make things clear. It is also upsetting to talk to the person as if they were a child and to discuss them with others in their presence.

Very few stroke patients are mentally confused. Spend as much time as possible with them, talk, listen and read to them and watch television, although not all the time, but remember they may only be able to cope with a little stimulation at a time. Look at pictures and photographs with them and encourage the patient to say what they can about them. Although the patient will get very tired at first, do invite their friends to visit them and also help them to pursue their old interests. A lot of time needs to be spent with the patient but this will help in restoring their speech.

Coventry Stroke Group is run completely by volunteers; none of us have any medical qualifications just common sense. We have our tea-ladies who do a wonderful job, they not only make the tea and coffee, but also help with any functions that entails the preparation of food etc., We are completely self funding, we pay for the ambulance which picks up people from their homes and returns them. Transport is our greatest expense, recently increased by Coventry City Council; we also pay for the room hire.

Working as a volunteer is very rewarding, particularly as you can see the stroke sufferers and their partners enjoying themselves and it does encourage them to come out of their homes and socialise. For some it is the only social event that they attend and they look forward to their fortnightly visit. All the activities we arrange are to try and help these people live as normal a life as possible and at the same time get fun out of the group.

Above: Celia Davies - second left.

Below: Beryl Hutchinson

Above: Joan McNally

Photo 1

Left:
Majorie Matthews

Above: Vera Hewitt in the farmyard at Piddlehinton

Photo 2

Above: Coventry National Women's Register members on a ramble

Below: Miranda Aston

Photo 3

Left:
Rosalie Berry

Below:
Mary Hart (right)
receiving a cheque
from Liz Millet on
behalf of Coventry
Building Society
Charitable Foundation.

Photo 4

Above: Muriel Hind pioneer motorcycle competitor.

Photo 5

Above: Ilse Wilson

Above:
Alice Lea standing at the back

Below: Suffragettes leaving Holloway Prison on their release

Photo 6

Memories of being a member of The Loyal Order Of Moose Coventry Lodge 102 Ladies Circle.

My membership of the Ladies Circle started when my husband joined the Lodge.

Doctor Wilson, a Scotsman who lived in America, studied the moose animal and saw how well they looked after their young and old and displayed the good qualities of family life, this made up his mind to form a society for members and their fellow men. James J. Davies who had emigrated to America as a child, always remembered his British roots, and in 1926, when he returned to his home town of Tredegar, he established the first Lodge in the U.K. From 1926 The Order grew steadily, enabling Moose members and their families to carry out humanitarian services both in the Lodge and the outside community.

Attached to each Lodge is a Ladies Circle, usually made up of wives or relatives of the Lodge members. They meet monthly, and annually the Circle elects its own officers and organises its own affairs within the guidelines of the Order. The Circle comprises of Lady Chairman, Vice Chairman, Secretary and Treasurer and all the ladies who normally organise and help with different functions. In the early days of the Circle it was considered the duty of the Ladies to have a rota to provide the lodge suppers for the men, because of this and the convenience of travelling the Ladies Circle inevitably met on the same night as the Lodge. Since those early days the Ladies have become involved in numerous activities for different charities and at times join with the men of the Social Committee and Community Service Committee (which are engaged in outside charity work) to help with whatever is needed.

One of the events which was held annually, was a dinner for people who were lonely and housebound, (this is a Community Service event), sometimes catering for as many as twenty-five people. This meal was held at the Lodge Room and the Brothers of the Lodge picked people up from their homes and returned them later. The Ladies cooked and served a three course hot meal, which was followed by entertainment. This was very rewarding, especially when someone said to you that they had not been out of their home for two or three years. Buffet Dances were also held at the Lodge Room and the Ladies were involved dealing with the menu and preparing the food. Each year a Strawberry Tea took place, usually in one of the member's gardens if the weather was fine, otherwise it had to be held in the person's house. In the past the strawberries and cream were donated by a relative of one of the members. The Ladies used to bake scones for this event. American Suppers were held in the Lodge Room (this is where everyone took a plate of food and it is shared). All these occasions were charity events.

Some time ago Hot Pot Suppers were held at Baginton Village Hall, attracting fifty to a hundred people. The writer and her husband used to prepare and cook the vegetables and meat at home (I never want to peel pounds of potatoes again). We used a large army cooking pot and other pans to carry the food in our car, then dash to Baginton and keep it warm on their cooker until it was time to be served. It was a work of art getting it all dished out ready for the Ladies and Men to wait on the tables. We also held a Sausage and Mash Supper (once again loads of potatoes to cook and mash). These two events were popular and we made a lot of money towards our charities.

The Ladies Circle also held Whist Drives, Craft Fairs, and Jumble Sales to raise money. At one Jumble Sale, which was held at the Lodge Room, a customer asked if we could exchange a settee for an armchair (she wanted us to collect this from her home and at the same time deliver the chair). She was disappointed when we told her it was not possible. Another time when we had a number of blankets for sale, when the doors were opened (we were standing behind the trestle tables ready to sell the goods). In rushed the customers, dashed to the table with the blankets on, pushing it back, so that we were pinned against the wall by the crush. One person grabbed the blankets and virtually threw them at us, when we eventually emerged from under these, she said she wanted all of them as she had a lodging house. We were also given a lift-off pram body (without the wheels), this was in an immaculate condition and it was decided that rather than sell it as jumble for a few pence we would give it to St. Faith's Shelter in Warwick Road, which was a home for unmarried mothers and battered wives, for it to be used as a carry cot.

We used to rent a shop at the bottom of Hill Street from Coventry Council to hold our Nearly New Sales. The shop was always in a filthy state. We always had to go and clean it before it could be used, apart from it being a dirty place it was always good fun. We had to stop people bringing in shopping trolleys, as the trick was to leave the flap open on the top and we caught someone sliding items off the sales table straight into their trolley (accidentally, of course). Another time one of our Ladies put a lovely long evening dress on a coat hanger and hung it up. Well, three customers came in and we thought they were drunk, one was trying to hold the other one up, they eventually went out of the shop and would you believe it the dress had gone. Looking back they obviously were not drunk, but were distracting us whilst one of them stole the dress. It was common to be left with old wet shoes and the ones we had for sale taken. For all this, it was good fun and we made a lot of money from nothing. When we got back to our homes, it was straight in the shower and our clothes in the wash.

The Ladies used to help the men of the Lodge at Christmas time making up and distributing grocery parcels to the needy. At Easter, together with the men, we used to take daffodils to people living on their own and also to certain old peoples homes. At the Christmas Lodge, a three course Christmas Dinner was provided. A couple of the Ladies would cook the turkey and a joint of pork at home and bring it to the Lodge Room. Four of the Ladies, including the writer, always volunteered to go into the kitchen on this night to do the vegetables and trimmings and to dish the food up, while other ladies set the tables and served the meal. As it was only a small cooker, (and on this night you had men from other Lodges attending so there was quite a few meals to do), it was always difficult to keep everything cooking and hot, shuffling the pans about. On one occasion we had the vegetables on in big saucepans and we stood a wooden board on top of one of the pans and put on it the joint of pork, just to keep it warm. One of the Ladies lifted up the board to see how the vegetables were doing and the pork fell down the back of the cooker and got wedged. There was a panic, we got a piece of wood and pushed the joint down, fortunately, it was a cooker with legs so we could retrieve it from the bottom. We gave it a good clean and nobody was any the wiser. Everyone enjoyed his or her meal!

The Ladies also organised a Travelling Supper (this is where you go to different peoples houses for each course). Four of us decided that we should do a trial run to see how long it would take to drive between the courses, and how much time would be required to eat the food, so off we went. When we got to one house, where they had said they would do a course, the gentleman was gardening and his wife was looking out of the window. The look on their faces was of devastation; they looked at each other, then at us in the car. We explained to them what we were doing, although they thought that we had arrived for a Social Committee Meeting or a Ladies Circle Meeting. All was resolved and we had a coffee with them. This supper was great fun; the writer did the main course, but attended all the other houses, so as not to miss out on anything, leaving the meal cooking. Unfortunately, as the Circle got bigger it was no longer possible to do this and we did not want to split it into two groups.

A highlight of the year was the 'Candlelight Supper,' this was held in the

Lodge Room, and was done in appreciation of the support given by the Ladies to the Lady Chairman. The room was set out with the tables in a square and covered with white tablecloths. In the middle of the square was a Candelabra on a small table and nightlights made to look like water lilies were on the tables. The Lady Chairman and her husband prepared and cooked a five-course meal at home and transported it to the Lodge Room. This was always an enjoyable evening.

The Ladies also helped with a trip to Twycross Zoo for underprivileged (or unruly as it turned out)) children from an area of Coventry. We hired a minibus and also used our cars. The Ladies made an assortment of sandwiches and cakes and took cans of pop. One of the men brought a big container of ice cream. The children gobbled the food up and we had to have eyes in the back of our heads to watch what they were up to. It was certainly an education, they might have lived in a deprived area but they were worldly wise. Anyway, they enjoyed themselves even if we were shattered.

One Christmas Eve afternoon we organised a party for the physically and mentally handicapped at a home in Weston under Wetherly. The Ladies prepared the food at home and provided each child with a Christmas stocking. We took the food along and put it on the tables. One of our Ladies who always made and decorated cakes beautifully, made a big cake in the form of a caterpillar; no sooner had it been put on the table, and our backs were turned the eyes had disappeared, one of the children had helped themselves. This was a rewarding afternoon but very sad, for it made us think how lucky we were.

The Ladies knitted squares for blankets, which were in the Moose colours (maroon and pale blue), with the Moose motif on them. I think we knitted about fifteen of these, and they looked very smart all being in the same colour. They were presented to a home for the elderly in Coventry and were much appreciated.

The highlight of the Ladies Circle year was the 'Ladies Evening'. This was held at a Hotel and for once the women did not have to prepare the meal themselves, it was very formal occasion. The Ladies wore long evening dresses and the men in dress suits all looking very smart. This was the evening when the cheques were given to nominated charities. The Ladies Circle having previously discussed which charities they would give a donation to. One time when the writer was Lady Chairman and her husband Governor the "Ladies Evening" was held at The De Montfort Hotel, Kenilworth. I was sitting on the top table next to the Lord Mayor, and as we chatted, I prepared to take a spoonful of my soup. On looking down I noticed to my horror that my Badge of Office had dropped off my collar and into the bowl of soup. I discreetly picked it out, wiped it on my serviette and put it back on my collar. (The soup still tasted good)!!!!

At one time there were two Lodges in Coventry Lodge 102 and 198. In 1985 they joined together and became Coventry Lodge 34. After being in the organisation for a number of years my husband and I had to resign due to business commitments. During this time we met and became friends with a lot of people, who we still have contact with. I can only say that I had some wonderful times, working hard with lovely genuine people, who were working together to help people less fortunate than themselves.

~~~~~~~~~~~~~~~~~~~~~~~~~~~~

The National Women's Register

Betty Jerman, a journalist with a young family, wrote an article about living in the suburbs with young children, which was published in the Guardian newspaper's 'Mainly for Women' page on 19th February 1960. She described the isolation experienced by intelligent women living in the suburbs, who probably held demanding jobs before embarking on motherhood. Mary Stott was editor of the Guardian's women's page at the time and fully supported the sentiments expressed by Betty Jerman. That article sparked off a reaction in Maureen Nicol, who was suffering exactly the same frustration at being tied to the home with two small children, very little money and no cultural stimulation. She responded by writing a letter to the Guardian, published just one week after the article, asking if it was not possible to have a register of women nationally, to make contact with like-minded women in a new area.

The post Second World War period was probably unique in history for the widespread rebuilding programme being carried out following the destruction caused by the war. Slum clearance of town and city centres was part and parcel of the whole ethos of regeneration. Huge, sprawling suburban estates and new towns were designed to accommodate a displaced and growing population as quickly as possible. The priority was housing and the infrastructure of social amenities was sadly lacking. Community centres, libraries, parks and facilities for young mothers were non-existent on many estates. Even shopping could mean inconvenient bus rides or a long walk with a pram and toddlers.

During the war women had played a huge part in keeping the factories and services running smoothly and they enjoyed having an income at their disposal. When peace returned women were no longer prepared to give up their jobs when they married, besides which the country needed the skills they provided. Post war education grew with the rise in population. There was a huge investment in schools and universities, giving rise to greater opportunities for further education at all levels of society. It was just this generation of young women who responded to Maureen Nicol's plea for a register of women tied to the home by family commitments and subject to frequent moves due to their husband's work. What Maureen did not anticipate when she wrote that letter was that all those who wrote in response looked to her to start a register. At first she was overwhelmed by what she had started, but obviously being of a practical nature she began sorting the letters into geographical regions. Another young mother, living on the same Cheshire estate, who had read her letter in the Guardian, called by to offer help and between them they tackled the mountain of mail arriving daily through the door. She appointed regional organisers, judging who suited the role best from their letters and forwarded the letters to them for sorting and forming local groups.

From its inception the Register was aimed at putting women in touch with each other for social interaction and stimulating conversation. There were to be no political or religious affiliations, nor was it to be used as a pressure group. The members would meet in each others homes and keep away from domestic subjects for their discussions. Only tea and biscuits were to be provided for refreshments to prevent competition amongst members for their culinary skills. It was up to each individual group to decide on the subject of their meetings, what one found interesting another might find very boring. Often it was left to the hostess of that meeting to decide the topic and the others to do some research, so that a lively discussion could take place. Early on it was found that daytime meetings did not work well, with numerous young children running around distracting their mothers. Evening meetings became the norm, where they could have a complete break from children and dads could be left in charge of their offspring. Contact with a wider circle of friends must have helped lonely members through difficult times. Some members said it saved their sanity and even the lives of their children, for they could have been suffering from post-natal depression. These contacts led to baby-sitting circles, which helped couples to get out on their own. The need for a register was brought about by couples moving away from relatives who would normally have been there to help a young mother with advice, baby-sitting and companionship. However, a move to a new area of the country cut them off from that traditional network of support. As the

Register grew and developed, so women moving to other countries with their husband's work started groups in those countries. By the end of the 1960s the Register had spread to Canada, Australia and South Africa, with others following.

Initially the name Maureen Nicol used for the organisation was 'Liberal-minded Housebound Housewives' Register.' This was rather a convoluted phrase and was shortened to 'Housebound Wives' Register.' Even this title had connotations of disability or age about it and finally 'National Housewives' Register' became the chosen title and remained until 1987 when it was thought to be rather old fashioned and the name was changed to 'National Women's Register.' This had always been the title of the South African group, for the widespread use of domestic servants negated the term housewife. Other countries adopted different names too right from the beginning to distinguish them from the home country.

From early in the life of the Register, finances were a problem. In those days when wives had housekeeping money and a tight budget to adhere to, extra expense could be problematic. The cost of postage, although cheap at the time, would put strain upon any organiser's finances when letters were running into hundreds. All correspondents were asked to put in a stamped addressed envelope with every communication, but many did not comply with the request. By the end of 1960 Maureen suggested a one-shilling (5p) registration fee to be paid to the Local Organiser, of which 15% should be sent to her for expenses. As she was not keen on formalising the finances of the Register it did not always work very well and frequently no fees were paid to her. When Maureen relinquished the position of National Organiser and holder of the Register after two and a half years there were 4-5,000 members.

Maureen's successor put the Register on a more business-like footing, raising the subscription charges and producing two newsletters per year. The first four National Organisers ran the Register alone from their homes. It dominated their lives and was run with dedication and commitment as economically as possible. How they coped with the new correspondence, the newsletters, keeping in touch with the Area and Local Organisers as well as bringing up their young children, running a house and in a few cases doing a part-time job is hard to imagine. Initially all newsletters were duplicated by the National Organiser and then by a local commercial enterprise. This was long before the advent of computers and printers to speed up the operation. As membership grew larger and spread wider some grassroots members felt rather remote from the higher echelons of the organisation. They did not see why they had to pay subscriptions, when they considered that they received no direct benefits. For some it must have been a struggle to pay subscriptions at all. The chain of communication did not work well in some areas, despite a newsletter sent to Area Organisers for distribution to individual groups. For some reason they did not always get through to the ordinary members. This left them ignorant of what was happening in other regions, leading to a more insular approach. In fact some groups seceded from the Register when subscriptions were raised to cover costs.

It was not until 1967 that the first conference was held. This gave individuals a chance to meet members from other regions and exchange ideas and experiences of belonging to the Register. Only those attending the conference were able to vote for officers in the organisation, postal voting did not occur until 1980. Many members must have been excluded from attending by the cost or the difficulties of leaving young children. The opinions of members were canvassed through a survey to find out what they wanted from their involvement with the Register. The first circular appeared in 1967, as a means of communicating policy from the leaders to the Local Organiser. By then there were 8,000 members and around 140 letters a week to process. It was far too much responsibility for one woman to deal with and two took over to share the load in 1970; one responsible for the Register, the other to deal with new members and the newsletter. Subscriptions were raised to five shillings (25p) to pay for help in processing the vast quantities of paperwork involved. By 1973 those two became three, although only for a year as one resigned due to pressure of work.

No one seemed to want to put the organisation on a formal footing, with a constitution, elected officers and a salary for all the work the organisers put into keeping it running smoothly. It is understandable that there was a reluctance to change a formula that had worked so far and adhered to the principle of self-help in which it was conceived. However, it became a victim of its own success and it became obvious that there had to be changes. At the 1974 conference it was put to the membership that the Register needed to be formalised in order to protect the organisers from financial liabilities. A circular was sent out to the members to canvas their opinion, but only 1% answered. A group of fact-finders helped to explore possible avenues along which to proceed. Should they become a charity or a company, there were beneficial and detrimental points to both options on offer. There was some dissatisfaction amongst members with the proposals and a group was formed to fight change, but they did not have the day-to-day burden of running a growing organisation. Abusive letters were even sent to the National Organisers, which suggests that they were totally unaware of how onerous the office had become. This could have been due to a feeling of remoteness from the decision-making process or were they content with their cosy meetings and averse to change? Maybe there was a feeling of apathy and not wanting to get involved. Eventually after taking legal advice a constitution was drawn up with specified officers who made up the National Group to be paid an honorarium rather than a salary. It all went through surprisingly smoothly in the end and took effect from July 1976. The greatest hitch was realising that they had been liable for VAT for the past two years and owed Customs and Excise £600. An appeal was launched for a 50p donation from every group, but the debt was not cleared for more than two years. By 1977 subscriptions had risen to £1 to help cover costs.

The National Group consisted of 5-15 elected members who shared the responsibility of running the organisation and appointed the National Organiser. They served a 4-year maximum term with half retiring every two years, to keep continuity. They continued to meet in each other's houses despite living some distance apart. The round robin system was adopted to keep everyone informed of what was happening. Officers within the group covered all aspects of management, public relations and even had an archivist. An overseas co-ordinator was added in 1979-80.

The National Housewives' Register became a charity in 1980 with the three leading figures, Maureen Nicol, Betty Jerman and Mary Stott as Trustees. When they retired from their trusteeship they were made Honorary Life Members. By 1986 the organisation became a Charitable Company Limited by Guarantee. The Trustees then had a dual role as Trustee Directors under the Companies Act and Trustee under the Charitable Act. It was necessary to stand for re-election every two years. Trustees could number between three and five and by 1988 the maximum number was reached. These changes were probably forced upon them by the rising membership in the 1970s and the burden of VAT involved.

The 1980s began at a high point, numbers were continuing to rise reaching 24,000 by 1982. Overseas groups became affiliated to the British group in 1980, encompassing 28 countries two years later. In that year, 1982, a national office was acquired in Norwich with an administrator and part-time paid staff to deal with correspondence. Through publicity generated by the 25th anniversary of the Register in 1985, fifty new groups were created. The peak in members in 1982 was followed by a slow decline over the next six years, then a rapid loss of members from 20,000 in 1988 to 11,200 in 1992. What happened to cause this escalation in the downturn during those four years? This was a period of recession in the country and worldwide, leading to high inflation. The 1980s had been a decade of opportunity for women in the workplace. More women went out to work, delayed having children and concentrated on career opportunities. When the recession bit in the late 1980s more women sought jobs to supplement the family income and pay high mortgage commitments. Negative equity arrived, leading to greater pressure on household budgets and a reluctance to move to another area and lose money on a property, which was probably the family's greatest asset. Many women could not afford the time or expense of belonging to a national group.

To combat the loss of membership in the late 1980s and early 1990s new initiatives were explored to generate a revival of interest in the Register and its aims. The National Conference was organised by different local groups each year at universities, where accommodation for a weekend was reasonably priced and facilities available for large numbers. Alternating the venue between the north, the midlands and the south gave all an opportunity to attend occasionally, if not annually. In addition to the National Conference, day conferences, discussion lunches, mini conferences and regional evening meetings helped to stretch the members' ideas and stimulate new interests.

In 1992 the 'New Image' was launched as one of the initiatives of the Strategic Plan to boost the dramatic loss of membership during the previous four years. The idea involved more regionalisation, with Regional Organisers as another tier in the hierarchy of leadership, to create more interactivity between groups. Part of this strategy was to target areas for advertising in the hope of creating new groups. Raising the profile of the Register meant bringing it to the notice of the public in a more sophisticated way. The media had always been exploited to widen the network of members, but maybe they needed a more aggressive approach. Publicity went out both locally and nationally and guidance was offered to members on how to get the message across succinctly if interviewed. Lists of topics were sent out to Local Organisers in case they had run out of ideas for meetings. The Research Bank was created to help members to research topics for discussion.

Not all groups were interested in what was going on in the rest of the country. Some had become complacent with their cosy little group and perhaps not as welcoming to newcomers as they had been. One local midlands group ceased attending area events in 1993-4. When contacted to find out the reason, it was stated that they were not interested in the regional or national situation and seceded from the Register. If this was the attitude of one local group, was it a widespread phenomenon? It certainly indicates a degree of selfishness, which was becoming more common after the 1980s.

It was in 1993 that direct mailing of the magazine 'The Register' to every paid-up member first began. It is a little confusing that the magazine was initially known as the newsletter, which kept members informed about what was going on in other areas. Direct mailing was a way of making sure that everyone was kept abreast of events and those that did not pay their subscriptions did not benefit from receiving one. Over the years the magazine has improved and developed into a full colour professional publication featuring articles written by the membership who send their contributions from all parts of Britain and affiliated groups abroad. The newsletter is now the replacement for the circular sent to the Local Organisers with information concerning the management and policy.

In 1980 there were 1,000 groups around the country, by 1991 that had reduced to 900. Subscriptions had been raised to £4 in 1990 and rose to £7.50 by 1992. By the end of the 1990s the decline had not stopped despite attracting more members steadily. For every new member joining, two were leaving. In 1998 Consultation Days were organised to address the problem of falling numbers. An ongoing process in the 1990s. In a letter to the Local Organisers of 1999 there is a tone of being under threat and encouraging them to make sure that all subscriptions were collected, as there was a strong belief that not all those attending meetings were paid up members. It was suggested that as many as 20% did not pay their dues. However, those just trying a few meetings out before deciding to join may have made up a proportion of that figure, as they were not expected to pay before sampling what was on offer. Investigation showed that only about 20% of those who made enquiries about joining actually did so.

In 1999 two new co-ordinators posts were created to tackle the issue, one for marketing and one for membership. The Marketing Co-ordinator dealt with publicity, media, public relations, editing the magazine and producing the newsletters. She also advised on the National Conference and maintained contact with overseas groups. The Membership Co-ordinator supported the members by visiting groups, attending meetings and events and creating strategies for encouraging new members. Part of that work was to evaluate the response of groups to new members and how they handled new enquiries. She also had the task of overseeing the office and attending Trustee meetings. At the same time that these changes in administration were taking place the office was reorganised. By 2001 Regional Organisers had been phased out, the co-ordinators having assumed much of their work. Office costs had been reduced as well as expenses for accommodation and meetings.

The efforts of the co-ordinators and their supporters paid off, for in 2000-2001 there was a rise in membership. Four new groups formed and two re-formed in that year. The finances have been helped by a grant from the Department of Education and Employment, which subsidises workshops and training courses for members. The introduction of Gift Aid in recent years has also helped to keep the current subscription to £13. The Annual Report of 2002 states that advertising is more important than ever. Word of mouth, broadcasting and leafleting targeted areas all play a part in bringing the Register to the notice of potential members. A website has also brought the organisation into the new millennium, tapping all sources of communication with the modern woman.

There have always been a variety of benefits in belonging to the Register, supplementary to the meetings, the friendship, outings and events. The House Swap scheme began in 1968 to help members take a cheap holiday without the expense of a hotel, guesthouse, etc. StAR, previously called Swap a Student, was created to help the children of members embarking on university or college life, who might need a bed for the night while attending an interview. The Postal Book Scheme began in 1986 for those who love to read, where 12 members from all over the country combine to form a group, select a favourite book from their own shelves and send it on to the next person in the group. Each member makes a comment in a notebook after reading it and sends it on again at the end of a month. It takes a year for the twelve books to get through the hands of the members and each book returns to its owner. The whole process begins again with a new selection of favourites. The Correspondence Magazine started in 1975 and contains a collection of letters from a small group, which excites lively discussion and friendship. Another scheme run on a one-to-one basis is the Penfriend Scheme, which began in 1991 for women who enjoy writing letters, but want a more personal correspondent.

The outlook for the future of the Register is good. It has changed and developed over four decades from the majority consisting of young mothers to a membership of mainly middle aged and older women. It has had to evolve to survive in the modern world. No longer are women tied to the home, without communications and transport, instead they are more commonly out at work and their young children, if they have any, being cared for by child minders or in nurseries. The need for companionship and stimulation has shifted to the older generation whose children have left the family home, who perhaps have retired from work or are working less, although younger mothers are always welcome. As long as women are willing to volunteer as Local Organisers and the programme of local and national events are as stimulating as they are at present, there will always be a place for the National Women's Register.

The Coventry Branch of the NWR

Muriel Allen initially belonged to Women in Touch (the Zimbabwe name for the NWR), as the classic member in the 1960s and 1970s with a young child, who needed more intellectual stimulation. When she moved to England with her family and settled in Coventry she looked for the nearest NHR(as it was then) group to join as a means of getting to know people in the area. Despite the size of the city she found that there was no group, so she and a friend Gill Bryant attended meetings in Kenilworth. After a year or so they decided that it would be far more convenient if they could interest the women of Coventry in setting up a group within the city. Muriel was instrumental in its foundation in 1979 and became the first Local Organiser after advertising for members to come along to a meeting. Initially there were only 4-6 members, but less than two years later they combined their efforts with the Kenilworth group to organise the 1981 National Conference at Warwick University for 300 members, with Professor E Laithwaite as the chief lecturer. This meant a huge amount of work for all involved in the process, but it proved just how capable these women were.

Although the Coventry group was small at the beginning, the membership rose steadily to more than a dozen. By 1980 there was talk of setting up a second group as it was thought to be growing too large to be accommodated in the average house, but nothing came of it. There was a fairly wide range of ages, from young mothers to older women. However, the criterion was not age but a lively mind and a willingness to participate. There was a good social mixture, with some working and some at home. Muriel remembers the meetings as being great fun and feels that she benefited greatly from her membership of the group. She has since moved on to other interests, but looks back with appreciation to her time with NWR.

Another founder member was Joy Bromfield who heard about the group from Muriel, a neighbour of hers. She was part of the team involved in hosting the National Conference in 1981 and particularly remembers the 10th anniversary celebration held on 3rd July 1989. Lyn Sutherland was the Local Organiser at the time, who put a great deal of effort into gathering together twenty-four members, past and present, to join the party at a local hotel and invited Mary Stott, one of the original trustees, to join them as a guest. It was a great compliment to the group when she accepted. The celebration nearly turned to disaster, however, when the hotel did not provide enough food. Apart from this hitch, all went well and it was an occasion which has lived in the memory of all those who attended. Joy has found it a friendly and lively group to belong to and has enjoyed her long membership.

When Anne Thompson, the present Local Organiser for Coventry, joined the NHR in 1985 there was a daytime group, as well as the usual evening meeting. This was one of the initiatives introduced by Lyn Sutherland. Those with young children met up for social interaction involving the children, separate from the more intellectual evening discussions. That no longer exists as children have grown and more women work away from the home. Playgroups and nurseries are more widely available and a mother and toddler group would serve the same purpose and give the children more space. Eileen Larssen was another Local Organiser who ran the group between Lyn and Anne, sometimes two women administering it together. Eileen put a lot of effort into keeping the group running successfully, but sadly died in 1998 as a result of breast cancer. Anne has been Local Organiser for about five years, attending consultation meetings, organising the programme and liasing with other areas, despite working full-time. She feels that there is far more liaison from top to bottom of the organisation than in the past. There is no fixed term of office, but when a Local Organiser decides to stand down, another is elected from amongst the members.

The youngest member of the Coventry group, Cathy McKay, joined in 1992 after reading an article about the NWR in a magazine. Feeling lonely in Coventry after moving from France, she tried the WI, but found it unsuitable. However, when she rang the number of the NWR and attended a meeting, she joined immediately as she found the members so friendly and welcoming. That first meeting coincided with Christmas celebrations, which she found particularly entertaining. Over the years numbers have fluctuated as women have joined, stayed for a while and moved on. Cathy found that a high proportion of members were not Coventry born, reflecting the original concept of helping women to settle in a new place. She now has children and a part-time job, making it difficult for her to make time for regular meetings. Despite her busy lifestyle she still belongs to the group and attends events and joins the outings when time and commitments allow. She has benefited from the support and friendship of other members over the years.

The Coventry group has enjoyed a varied programme of topics for discussion at its meetings over the past twenty-four years. Events have included social evenings, quizzes, a French course, Open University courses, walks, theatre visits, day trips, workshops and many more. The members took part in a Medieval Conference recently, organised locally. There are so many advantages to belonging to the NWR, it is surprising that numbers are not higher. It would be interesting to know what the members are planning for their twenty-fifth anniversary next year.

Acknowledgements
Special thanks go to Anne Thompson for all her help and information. For the loan of documents, letters, magazines and Betty Jerman's book.
Also thank you to Muriel Allen, Joy Bromfield and Cathy McKay for allowing me to interview them.

Bibliography
The Lively-Minded Women: The First Twenty Years of the National Women's Register, by Betty Jerman.
The Register Magazines and newsletters.

~~~~~~~~~~~~~~~~~~~~~~~~~~~~

Mary Hart

Wyken Adventure Centre was first set up in 1994 by three Neighbourhood Watch Co-ordinators, of which Mary Hart was the chairman. They saw the need for the provision of 'activities for the young people who had little to do in the evenings'. The aim of those concerned was to provide access to sporting activities at an affordable cost to the families. The outcome was a successful adventure centre, run and managed by volunteers, which was later granted charitable status.

Mary Hart was born in Kenilworth, but has spent most of her life in Coventry apart from a brief period in Devon where she and her husband set up in business. For health reasons Mary was advised to leave that county so the family returned to Coventry. However, she has not ruled out retiring there.

Back in the city Mary set up a business employing staff for the motor industry, but had to give it up after suffering injuries in a car accident. To keep herself occupied she returned to education and studied several subjects gaining qualifications as a nursery nurse (NNEB) and a Certificate in Education. Mary then attended Wyken Adult Education Classes in Information Technology. This year she has completed a course in leadership through the Common Purpose programme.

It was while studying at the Education Centre that Mary had been approached to become the co-ordinator for the Neighbourhood Watch Scheme. This was a voluntary post and she has been the Chairperson for fourteen years. Owing to the essence of the work Mary became aware of the amount of crime, especially juvenile crime, in the area. This set her thinking that if the youngsters were kept occupied their anti-social behaviour would lessen. She was certain that given something constructive to do the young people would respond and the local residents too, would benefit. A suitable building was already available on the estate.

The Wyken Community Centre building was under used, so Mary wrote to the council's Community Education Department only to receive a negative reply. Apparently they were closing down community centres not leasing them out. Undaunted by this she was determined not to let her project drop.

It was some time later that Mary received an invitation to a meeting of people, from both the voluntary and statutory sectors, to discuss future usage of the centre. She took along her husband and another co-ordinator, together with other interested parties. The outcome was that with support from a local authority funding officer they applied for a 'pot of money' from the lottery.

The bid was unsuccessful with no reason given. Nevertheless, in 1992 the Wyken PIE Project was born, fore-runner of Wyken Adventure Centre. The abbreviation PIE stood for Participation, Investment and Encouragement and was the title used initially when applying for funding. The project received the support of the police, the local Member of Parliament and the city leisure services. Their local councillor Joan Wright was particularly encouraging throughout.

The new club had started with support from the Open Award Centre which offered trainees and a leader. A dri-ski slope was built using equipment which had been in store and children of the members built and painted it. Meanwhile a wall was built for abseiling practice. Again support came from the Open Award Centre who supplied trained personnel and loaned equipment for abseiling and archery. Later the Police Community Initiative Fund awarded a grant of £1000 which was used to purchase harnesses for the abseiling venture, rather than continue to use those on loan.

The children in the area were enthusiastic and advertised the club, either by word of mouth or distributing leaflets in their schools, with the permission of their Head Teachers. These same young people re-named the club Wyken Adventure Centre (WAC) and membership cards were issued. Attendances at the centre grew, from the four to six children who 'kicked a ball around'. The club was open on four evenings a week and a charge of fifty pence for the two-hour sessions was made.

Mary's experience of management and administration meant that she was able to offer her skills for the benefit of all. Setting up the venture meant that several issues had to be addressed, such as police checks for all those aged eighteen and over, in the interests of child protection. Other areas covered were health and safety, fire safety, first aid, insurance risk assessment for all activities and food hygiene. Notices, confirming that all categories covered, had to be publicly displayed.

Raising money was essential if the club was to improve and attract more people. Unfortunately, it soon became apparent that no resources were available, to improve the thirty rooms in the community centre building, despite them not having 'seen a lick of paint in as many years'! This decision was unacceptable to the committee, for the building was a good strong one; too good to be left to dereliction. They therefore decided to operate alone, voluntarily, but with the support of the Open Award Centre whose advisers were available to offer help and advice when consulted. Community Education dealt with specific problems.

There was little heating and only one toilet available in the building, while the membership of WAC was increasing greatly, even more so than had been anticipated. Although Community Education paid the overheads and allowed the club rent-free usage for several years, there was no money forthcoming for improving the fabric of the building which was in a state of disrepair. However, among the members of the centre were those with the necessary skills who were willing to use them to upgrade the building. The work was undertaken by these volunteers which resulted in major internal improvements. A Pool Room was built by adults serving Community Service Orders, working under the supervision of Probation Officers. Structural improvements, together with plumbing and electrical work, had to be carried out by local authority approved contractors.

Help also came from an unexpected quarter when Community Education approached the centre to discuss the feasibility of using the main hall for the use of Adults with Learning Difficulties. In order to enable them to have access to activities suited to their needs, the building had to be made available to them during the daytime. To fulfil current legislation covering the disabled, Community Education financed new toilet facilities, upgraded the lighting and refurbished emergency equipment.

Meanwhile a management committee had been formed to run the centre and organise a fund raising programme. Willing members can only do so much and finding the money to buy the necessary equipment became ongoing. Mary had not had experience of fund raising, but soon learned the art. She began by sending out letters asking for support and putting in bids for small amounts of money. Fund raising then began in earnest and during the first five years of its existence the centre received grants from various local organisations. This enabled the number and type of activities offered to be increased and to train those interested, both the young and their parents, to become actively involved with the centre.

Taking on such an old building meant that frequent refurbishing needed to be carried out. Fortunately there are a large number of concerns willing to sponsor groups in need of money. The heavy use of equipment, used in the many activities undertaken at the centre, means it has to be replaced from time to time to keep up with the required health and safety regulations.

Mary put in several successful bids for small amounts of money. She also applied to the Variety Club of Great Britain for a grant through Tesco's store in Dorchester Way (Coventry). To support the application Mary had to compile a portfolio, covering the activities undertaken at WAC, and answer many questions about the club. Against competition, from other organisations across the country, the application was successful and WAC received an award of £8000, the highest donation they had ever received.

'Between 2000 and 2001 we [WAC] worked in partnership with Community Education, Wyken Community Centre and Wyken Youth Team to refurbish a store to make it into a Dark Room'. The costs were shared and WAC volunteer painters and carpenters completed the project.

The following year an application to the Heart of England Community Foundation resulted in the generous grant of £5000 being given. This went towards making an old store into a 'Tuck Den', a name suggested by the children. Fire doors were installed as were extractor fans heating, lighting and carpeting. After the room was painted it provided a 'much needed resource which the children love'.

The Health Improvement Programme (HIP) gave £500 which funded short tennis. As the sport and leisure activities on offer have grown so has the membership. Mary has been able to arrange short trips and adventure holidays, for the young people of WAC, many of whom would not have been able to have afforded a holiday.

Such is the spirit engendered by the Centre that its members work with the Residents' Association and other agencies to improve the area. National Spring Clean Week held in 1997 was supported by schools, residents' associations and community groups across the city. According to the

Coventry Evening Telegraph (21/04/97), the Lord Mayor, 'Councillor Stan Hodson swopped his chain of office for broom and duster' when launching the event from WAC.

Supported by the city council's environmental scheme and encouraged by the presence of a later Lord Mayor, Sheila Collins, the children worked enthusiastically with organised clean-ups on the estate. The first doorstep paper and cardboard recycling scheme was also set up there and launched by the Belgrave Residents' Neighbourhood Watch Association (BRANWA) of which Mary is the Chairperson. These achievements are the result of Mary's commitment to both groups over the years. Most grants were 'one-off' donations, but BRANWA became fully involved in community projects and worked together constantly to raise money for the centre. In 1998 they donated £150, to add to the £1000 from WAC's own funds, towards the construction of a greenhouse for the use of the Adults with Learning Difficulties. However, the residents also remembered other needy children and donated £150 to the Snowball Appeal run by the Coventry *Evening Telegraph*.

Over the years that the club has been established there has been a huge change in the use of the centre and club itself. Volunteers take complete responsibility for its running and general maintenance. In the early days the activities offered were very limited, but attendance has grown, from six young people in 1992 to over 600 registered members whose ages range from five years old to twenty plus. In 2002 four leaders and eight children were sent on a four-day trip to Dol-Y-Moch Outward Bound Adventure Centre. The activities there complemented those back at the Wyken Centre, but also included canoeing, caving and trekking. Once again the visit was made possible through grants received from Coventry Building Society, the Forester's Fund for Children and Sports Award for all.

The centre was able to offer Millennium Volunteer Awards, financed by Coventry Voluntary Service Council (CVSC), to young people who worked voluntarily at the centre providing them with training, travel allowances and clothes.

During the last twelve months Mary has worked with CVSC to obtain Charitable status for the club, which was successful. On this basis she wrote to the Town and Country Festival organisers requesting that they might support their group. Thus, they nominated WAC as one of their chosen charities for the year, and gave them space to hold a display and show a video advertising their activities. The stall raised £217 and WAC was also given £1500 by the festival organisers.

Membership of the centre is slowing down as the costs of using it increases. 'We have to pay our way' says Mary. 'We are, in effect, a victim of our own success. I have been able to raise money for all of the activities we offer, including the replacement of equipment and also for training staff. We have a full compliment of music and disco equipment. We also have a computer room'.

Mary gratefully admits that it is only through the generosity of their sponsors' belief in them, that they are able to continue and increase the number of activities on offer. As a charity it relies wholly on volunteers. Despite health problems Mary continues her work and has the satisfaction of knowing that crime figures for the area have been reduced since the inception of Wyken Adventure Centre.

Marjorie Matthews
Allesley Hall Community Centre

Although Marjorie Blythe was born in Sunderland she came to Coventry when she was four and a half, her mother having been directed to work at an ammunition factory in the city. Her father was in the army. The family lived in Hugh Road, Stoke, and Marjorie attended a small Church of England school on Stoke Green moving on to Stoke Council School in Briton Road. While still at school she met her future husband Robert Matthews and the couple married in 1958. Housing was not too plentiful at that time so their first home was a rented flat above the shop of Marjorie's parents where in 1960 Lynne, the first of their three children, was born. By the time they had their second daughter, Tracey, Marjorie and Robert had started to buy a house in Hugh Road. However they later moved to Allesley Park where, in 1967, a son Lee completed the family.

Because her eight year old daughter complained that she was bored Marjorie, together with another parent Therese Hodges, approached the community centre to ask whether they could run a youth club for juniors. They went to a meeting of the Allesley Park committee and were given permission, provided one of them joined the committee. They would also be required to do their own funding. So the two women set to and collected enough items to enable them to hold a jumble sale.

It was decided to open the club on a Wednesday evening for two hours from seven o'clock. About forty children turned up on the first night, but membership grew rapidly until the centre had a membership of about a hundred children. Various activities were laid on to occupy them and gradually the activities offered increased. Discos were popular and a good source of revenue. A stage was built in the youth club and plays were produced. The entrance charge levied raised money to keep the club going. Saturday morning film shows too, were well attended. A senior youth club, a women's club and a playschool were already in existence and the centre proved to be a useful venue for occasional meetings for various groups.

Marjorie joined the committee which consisted mainly of men at that time. The community centre had to be self-supporting and although only a 'peppercorn rent' was paid, the building had to be maintained and it always needed funds. Consequently, raising money was to be the most important item on the agenda and continues to be. Marjorie has always made this her prime concern.

The original committee used to organise fairs in the local field and a carnival was added which Marjorie undertook to arrange. It paraded round the Allesley Park Estate. Eventually she 'just drifted' into becoming the Chairman. The carnivals continued for sixteen years, but it became increasingly difficult to get volunteers to help. Each year the event cost more to run as marquees had to be hired. The committee decided to abandon such large events and stopped organising them. Marjorie attempted to run a community centre based carnival and fair, but after a while this too, proved too onerous for the few who volunteered their services and they were discontinued. Marjorie also served on the Coventry Carnival Committee with another member of the community centre.

In 1987 on the night of the 14th November, an inauspicious for Coventrians, Marjorie was called from her home because the youth club building was on fire. It was completely destroyed, but fortunately the flames were kept away from the explosive materials stored by the Coventry Parks Department in a building in dangerously close proximity.

On the following Sunday the committee met to consider the repercussions of the event. It was feared that they were not fully covered by insurance and would be responsible for the cost of rebuilding. Fortunately this was not the case, the city council had insurance however it only provided three-quarters of the money needed. Without wasting time, as a start, it was decided to 'sell' bricks to the residents of Allesley Park towards raising the money for rebuilding the youth club. This was eventually done and the young people still had somewhere to go. As is usual in insurance cases the building had to be rebuilt to the original plans, but the inside was modernised making the room far more useful. Offices were added and gradually other refinements such as carpeting, thus enabling the centre to increase the recreational activities. Yoga and a Ladies' Keep Fit class was started and the room was let for children's parties. Two rooms had then been modernised.

Coventry Gardens Department vacated a room, which they had occupied and left in a very dilapidated state, therefore it was decided to bring this into use which meant more fundraising. An education programme had been set up by the city council teaching building skills, so these workers renovated the room but the community centre committee had to pay for the work.

The centre has gone from strength to strength, but it has become financially harder to maintain the building despite the low rent. The women's club, now called The Thursday Club, and the playschool are still there and a pre-school playgroup has been established. The activities taking place have increased in number and now include bowls and rock and roll dancing.

Several education courses are being run such as painting classes, held both during the day and in the evening, and five language classes. An office was made available for the Education Department which had to pay for using the centre. As well as benefiting the wider community these courses are necessary to help the survival of community centres, run independently of schools. It is very difficult, such centres are much needed, but financial aid is not always forthcoming.

Having taken over land behind the community centre, backing onto the walled garden of Allesley Hall, members are in the process of laying out a 'Peace Garden', a wildlife garden and an area with glasshouses. During the day people with learning difficulties use the centre and it is proposed that they use the facilities to acquire gardening skills.

A group was set up by Marjorie which she named the Central Agency and its employees did woodworking and bricklaying. Run independently they carried out various decorating tasks for the elderly and paid for using the community centre as a base. The Agency became so successful that they decided to leave the centre and run their business independently.

Undeterred Marjorie set up a painting, decorating and handyman scheme. She employed three painters and two more men, on a part-time basis, who all went into the community carrying out tasks such as gardening, fencing and paving. This greatly assisted in keeping the community centre 'afloat,' together with the continuous fund raising.

Marjorie then joined a committee for the community centres of Coventry to find out how other centres were run. Most were council controlled and therefore received funding from the council, whereas other centres began each year not knowing how much money was available. She says that she was frequently 'knocked down' when speaking because of the difference in the way other centres were run. However, after many years things are changing. All the community centres in the city are now going to have to be self sufficient like Allesley Park.

Managers, cleaners and the playschool leaders at Allesley Hall Community Centre were all paid, but Marjorie worked voluntarily and because of this she was invited to an annual function given by the city council for voluntary workers. Having worked constantly to find money for running the community centre she deplored the amount of money spent on these occasions and stopped attending.

Besides bringing up three children, Marjorie worked in the evening collecting money for an agency. Always her main concern was that she was at home for her children. The voluntary work for the community centre was done from home.

Although thoroughly enjoying her involvement Marjorie says . . .

Doing the community centre [work] over the years has been great fun, but it is no longer fun it's business. The people using the centre now take it for granted, but like many organisations new recruits are not forthcoming. So many people work and cannot, or will not, find the time to serve the community, but are quite willing to attend social groups or the educational classes held there.

Marjorie is always mindful that one has to move with the times. She states that the year 2002 was the worst in her experience because of increasing legislation. No longer is a youth club the place solely for relaxation and games, dancing or pure socialising. Owing to new regulations governing what young people must be taught, such as drug awareness and other topics deemed essential for their betterment, it is virtually impossible to enlist adults to run them. Police checks, although important, add to the problems. While thoroughly in favour of increasing health and safety measures, fulfilling them is an expensive business. Money has been awarded for a soft play area for the younger children and further funding is anticipated to help complete the project. These, quite rightly have to meet special regulations concerning the type of equipment used both inside and out.

The committee, which is still wholly female, has many ideas for the future of the community centre and all of those involved are attending courses in carrying out administrative tasks, such as applying for grants, among other things. They attend these courses run by the Coventry Voluntary Service Council and are also in the process of making Allesley Park Community Centre a limited company. This will release the committee members from some responsibility such as standing as guarantors or having to find money urgently, often lending their own in an emergency. Such loans are always repaid. This is one aspect which deters younger people from offering their services, but this looks likely to change when the centre becomes a limited company. Several younger people appear interested in joining and playing a full part in the next phase.

Marjorie Matthews may have retired from Allesley Park Community Centre, but we have not heard the last of her. Perhaps it is her gipsy heritage that makes her restless. Although still committed to fund-raising for the centre voluntarily, she is looking to do some other worthwhile work perhaps with a political slant. Always straightforward, she is not one to stand by if she considers an injustice has been done and furthermore is not afraid to speak her mind. Accordingly Marjorie intends to 'take up the cudgel' on behalf of Coventry citizens and wants to make her views heard on the state of the city. When money is available she would like to see it spent on worthwhile schemes. For example many Coventry areas, including Allesley Park, could do with proper skateboarding facilities which would then take skateboarders off the streets where they constitute a danger.

Another issue about which Marjorie feels strongly is that of housebound people. She considers that important necessities are ignored. Former home helps' duties and titles have changed. They are now called Community Care Assistants and their work is mostly personal care.

Marjorie's involvement with the community centre in the early days caused minor friction at home. Her husband said 'One day you will have to choose between the community centre and us'. Now in his retirement he too, is a very keen volunteer there. Her late father was also involved for some years. Now that her daughter, Lynne, has taken over her mother's role Marjorie is delighted. It really is a 'family affair'.

The high esteem in which Marjorie is held was revealed when she finally retired. From the wonderful presents she received to the 'family dinner', which turned out to be a surprise gathering of many friends from Allesley Park, and yet more presents. In all Marjorie worked for thirty-five years at Allesley Park Community Centre. Asked what she enjoyed most about her long association with it Marjorie said 'I like meeting people and depending on how you approach them, most people are nice. I wouldn't change my life in any way. I've thoroughly enjoyed it'.

Marjorie was interviewed in October 2002

~~~~~~~~~~~~~~~~~~~~~~~~~~~~~~~

ROSALIE BERRY Née Clements

The aim of this research group is to celebrate the achievements of 'ordinary women'. Rosalie Berry would certainly have considered herself ordinary, but as her daughter, Diane says 'She was immensely talented and had such a wide variety of interests. She approached everything that she did with enormous enthusiasm which carried along those around her. She had a great spirit of fun loving nothing more than putting on a play or organising a dance, …'.

Rosalie certainly lived life to the full covering all aspects, the domestic, working and recreational. Whichever role she was fulfilling she never failed to give to it her full commitment. She was an inspiration to others and this profile shows that 'women can have it all' a happy and fulfilling marriage and an interesting and enjoyable life outside the home, both shared with a husband and independently.

Rosalie Clements was born in Hartshill, Nuneaton in a cottage which was once the home of an Elizabethan poet, Michael Drayton. She was one of seven children. Her father was a skilled factory worker and her mother a cook to a local family, but she was inclined to have 'itchy feet' so the family moved house frequently, between Coventry and Nuneaton, which of course, meant several changes of school for the children. Rosalie's final school was Broad Street Girls School, Coventry. On leaving there her head Teacher, Miss Ada Wade, wrote a testimony stating 'As regards character, Rosalie Clements is absolutely reliable. . . . She would, I am sure, give satisfaction in any work she undertakes.'

Rosalie left school at the age of fourteen and worked in the offices of several Coventry factories. While working at the Daimler Factory she met Sydney Berry to whom she was married for almost fifty years. Sadly he died just short of their Golden Wedding anniversary in 1997.

Rosalie stopped working when their daughter, Diane, was born. However, she kept herself busy making nearly all of her own and Diane's clothes. Having acquired her mother's culinary skills Rosalie thoroughly enjoyed cooking, especially for the large family gatherings she often held. Another of her interests was gardening. She was extremely knowledgeable about plants and liked to share her expertise. When I moved into an established garden she came and identified the plants for me as well as supplying me with others from time to time (I did not thank her for the Euphorbias which rather 'took over'!), but the others are a pleasant reminder of her.

In the 1960s Rosalie returned to work, initially on a part-time basis. She worked for Coventry City Council and from there she went as 'Correspondent to the Managers' of Newfield School in Kingfield Road, where she dealt with all the administrative matters including book-keeping. The school was for maladjusted girls and at the time was under the auspices of the Home Office, but when it came under the care of the local authority in 1972 Rosalie left. The chairman of the managers had been a Mr Liggins, whose family had a lingerie factory in Hillfields, so she went to work for him in an administrative position until the factory closed.

Rosalie was a great lover of animals, especially dogs, having kept

Sealyham Terriers, now out of general favour. She also kept a miniature Dachshund for several years and after it died she had a dog to puppy walk for the Guide Dogs Association. It was extremely lively and Rosalie said she kept finding articles, which it had chewed, for months after the dog had been returned for training. She was sent frequent reports regarding the dog's progress and was pleased to hear that it was proving to be a useful guide dog.

In the 1960s Rosalie was a member of the Townswomen's Guild (TWG), which met at St Christopher's School in Winsford Avenue, Coventry. The TWG had several sections including a weekly Arts and Crafts group, of which Rosalie was a member, for she was very adept with her hands and extremely artistic. A Social Studies group met monthly and members read papers on a chosen subject. Both groups combined occasionally with area TWGs to produce exhibitions open to the public and Rosalie was always concerned with the organisation of such events.. For several years she also attended painting classes and her home contained many of her small watercolour prints which included butterflies and flowers. One knowledgeable visitor asked if one of her paintings was a Monet print!

For financial reasons the TWG members decided to leave the organisation, to join the National Association of Women's Clubs (NAWC). The club became known as The Winsford Club. Rosalie became secretary and also represented the NAWC at monthly area meetings. The post of secretary is undoubtedly the most onerous task on any committee and, using her administrative experience, she carried out her duties enthusiastically and efficiently. The subsections included drama and Annual Drama Festivals were held in which Rosalie participated. One club member wrote a play for the event. As usual Rosalie played a part and, most satisfyingly, the Winsford Club won the competition.

The Social Studies group continued and when the NAWC folded, owing to lack of members, twelve women including Rosalie, continued meeting. Meetings were held at members' houses where the host provided refreshments. Although Rosalie later developed diabetes this did not deter her from providing sumptuous cakes, even when it had been decreed 'biscuits only'. Her whole contribution to the group was greatly missed when she died.

Rosalie's métier was The University of the Third Age (U3A). An idea instigated in Toulouse, France. In 1985 a meeting was held at the Technical College, now the City College, with the aim of setting up a U3A. The first two ages being childhood and work. It was recognised that those no longer in full-time employment had resources and skills which could be used to their mutual benefit in educational and cultural activities. No educational qualifications are required, but it is expected that members become both learners and teachers. Within each U3A like-minded people get together and form smaller groups led by one of its members. All contribute to any costs arising from their use of educational or cultural facilities. Individual groups meet regularly, and also the whole membership attend meetings together throughout the year.

Rosalie attended the inaugural meeting becoming a founder member of the Coventry U3A and serving as Chairman for two spells. Such was her enthusiasm that she joined several groups and was instrumental, with another member, of forming a choir which sang for pleasure and occasionally entertained outside the U3A. Rosalie also joined the play-reading group and was influential in locating the Cheylesmore Community Centre for meetings. The U3A raised money towards curtains for the stage which benefited both them and the centre. For many years the ramblers produced a pantomime, written by Rosalie, which was performed at the Christmas gathering of all members.

Her husband Syd became a member of the rambling group and planned the routes for their twice-weekly rambles plus the 'pub' to which they would return for lunch! Soon afterwards Rosalie also joined and became the secretary, a post she continued to hold even after she was unable to undertake the walks. The group also went on walking holidays both in this country and abroad which Rosalie and Syd thoroughly enjoyed. Such is the camaraderie of members that when Syd was taken very ill on one such holiday, in Cheshire, Rosalie was invited to stay with a former Coventry member living close by who looked after her, taking her to visit Syd in hospital. Happily, he duly recovered enough to continue his full participation in the U3A.

Rosalie was involved in organising a successful pageant at St Mary's Hall celebrating the tenth anniversary of Coventry U3A.

The subject which most interested Rosalie and her husband was local history. They both participated fully on joining this group and from 1987 until 1992 Rosalie was the Chairperson. 'She was excellent at this and no one did it better' states Elizabeth Haycock the Group Leader at that time. Rosalie and Syd were also frequently to be found preparing refreshments for various group social occasions throughout the year. Besides having speakers at their meetings, the members went on visits to places of interest covering a wide local area. Gradually the areas covered were extended to take in neighbouring counties. For several years Syd helped to organise visits, together with the Group Leader, who says 'We always had to have lunch at a Banks's pub, (Syd's choice)'. After Syd died, to her credit and despite her own gradually failing health, Rosalie continued his work organising local history trails, planning and visiting the proposed area, together with Elizabeth. This was done most meticulously, reading about them, planning the route, transport and personally going on a 'recce' before taking members out. They chose pubs for lunch with care always trying to keep the cost below £5 per head! Elizabeth says they had 'great fun' preparing the visits.

It was only when Elizabeth moved away from the city, and no one volunteered to take her place, that Rosalie regrettably decided that she too must give up the organising. Nevertheless she continued as Group Leader finding speakers for the monthly meetings.

The esteem in which Rosalie was held was evident in the size of the congregation at her funeral and the subsequent gathering which followed. This last, took place at the allotment building in Westwood Heath, a venue where' she had spent many happy times. Fittingly it was the most beautiful sunny, winter's day. Tributes were paid to her and glasses raised in remembrance of a woman who had lived life to the full and would be greatly missed by many. Though tinged with sadness it was a most joyous, occasion.

My thanks to Diane Aderyn, Rosalie's daughter, for her help.

Thanks also to U3A members, Joyce Hogben, Dorothy Simpson and Elizabeth Haycock for sharing their memories of Rosalie.

~~~~~~~~~~~~~~~~~~~~~~~~~~~~~

ILSE WILSON

Ilse Wilson, nee Rath, was born in Danzig, Germany, in 1933 and came to live in Coventry, on marrying in 1959. She describes her early childhood as idyllic, with happy memories of walking to school with friends through a little wood, playing imaginative games. Sometimes she walked with her father as he made his way to work. Winter snow brought its own delights as the local children skied or tobogganed on nearby hills. They played until it was beginning to get dark, ignoring calls from mothers to go inside although 'our mittens were frozen stiff on our painfully cold hands'.

In contrast, summer holidays were taken on the Baltic coast where Ilse remembers spending 'every day under a cloudless sky, on seemingly endless beaches of snow white sand . . . I remember the tears of pain when the sand burned the soles of my feet'. However, war was imminent and Ilse's life was to change dramatically.

For those of us who lived through the Second World War it is hardly necessary to be reminded of the trauma of frequent air raids. Undoubtedly neither we, nor the families in Germany gave any thought to each other's sufferings during the long conflict.

The scenario for the Rath family mirrored our own. As night after night the sirens sounded their warning of an impending raid, Ilse's mother would waken her children and take them down into the cellar. They returned to their comfortable beds on hearing the 'All Clear' signal, but so often was the family disturbed it was eventually decided that they should remain in the cellar until morning, when the bombing ceased.

The war totally devastated the family home and the city of Berlin. Ilse and her family became separated, never to be a complete family again. They endured years of privation and anguish, from which they never fully recovered.

One of the worst eras was during the closing months of the war (1945) when the invasion was heralded by the continuous sound of sirens. Although people had stockpiled food in preparation, fresh food was hard to obtain. Ilse says 'We ate potatoes and Swedes until the sight of them made my robust constitution protest'. This was made worse by the fact that the potatoes had been affected by frost and 'had the sweet smelling stench of rotting vegetation, but we had to eat them in order to survive. Nothing that was edible was ever thrown away'. Meals would frequently consist of the tough outer leaves of cabbage, vegetable peelings and pea pods. Her mother reminded the children that 'hunger makes the best chef'. This situation continued for some time, until gradually bread and vegetables started to appear in the shops once more. However queuing was necessary, often for hours, without any guarantee that there would be any commodity left to buy.

The unsettling war, and immediate post war years, had forced Ilse to change schools eight times, and temporary accommodation fourteen times. After leaving school at the age of seventeen and a half she came to England in 1950 to start a career in curative education in Bristol. She trained in Scotland where she worked for two shillings pocket money a week, on a voluntary basis, in an independent boarding school for children in need of special care. She was a teacher and house parent on duty for twenty-four hours a day with one half day off in seven days. When there was a staff shortage, she also managed to cook for ninety people.

After three years, Ilse's work took her to Dublin to a family where she was governess to their mentally disturbed, five year old son. They travelled between Dublin and London, where in Hampstead, the child was treated at the Anna Freud Clinic and Ilse worked in liaison with the resident psychiatrist. After leaving this family she took over a very small, privately run school for mentally and physically handicapped children, which was based in an outbuilding in the London garden of a Russian psychologist. The income from that school was poor and Ilse received a wage which was barely enough to pay the rent for a furnished room. She was always hungry, overworked and lonely.

Totally exhausted, she interrupted her work after five years and took a post-graduate course in Art and Crafts in Dusseldorf. With the extra qualification she returned to a boarding school for maladjusted children, in Northamptonshire, again on an unpaid basis. There she met her future husband, David.

Ilse and David started married life 'without a penny to their name' and lived with his parents in Coventry. They moved to rented accommodation before finally settling in their own home in Earlsdon. There they brought up three children under difficult circumstances, as two of the children, the eldest and the youngest, suffered from a genetic, unidentified, and therefore untreatable, skin condition which needed constant care and attention. Visits to the local hospital and Great Ormond Street Hospital, in London, and the experimental medication prescribed made the children suffer and their condition worse. Diets and two long stays at a sanatorium in the Black forest area of Germany were stressful for all concerned and merely raised false hopes.

Life revolved around the children and left time for little else. Just as creativity and music had played a great part in Ilse's early years, so she encouraged her children's artistic and musical talents. All three of them learned to play the piano and Nicola, the youngest, later played the flute and graduated from university with a degree in music. Ilse also managed to squeeze in some art courses for herself and she joined the Choir of the Saint Michael Singers in Coventry Cathedral, under their conductor, David Lepine and later Robert Weddell. Her first task was to translate the 'German Requiem' by Brahms into English and teach the Choir the German pronunciation of the work. David Lepine was a perfectionist and the work had to be sung with understanding at the next concert.

During that time Ilse was also asked by the Canon of the Cathedral to translate the *'Rules of Taizé'* from the English into German. The Taizé Community is a retreat in Burgundy. 'Young people from all over the world seek out this place of reconciliation and peace. It is made up of Brothers of Catholic and non-Catholic origin'. The Canon then took the translation to the Benedictine Monastery in Ottobeuren, in Germany.

At Christmas 1973 Ilse and David's eldest son Marcus was struck down with leukaemia. He was thirteen years old. Three years later Ilse decided to train as a nurse at Walsgrave Hospital where, after a six-year battle against leukaemia, Marcus died. Ilse wrote his life story, which she published and sold, with the aim of helping other sufferers from the disease. Together with the money raised from a musical concert, £2000 was given to the hospital to buy equipment for the leukaemia ward. Ilse continued nursing until her retirement in 1993.

From then on Ilse devoted her time to writing her life story and putting into print her extensive correspondence with her parents, spanning the years 1950 1983. She joined a 'Creative Writing' course and began painting with watercolours. She also joined several gardening clubs and finds peace and contentment in her own 'busy' garden. Occasionally she helps a friend who has a nursery for unusual plants.

Now retired, both Ilse and her husband attend talks and lectures on a variety of subjects. They are members of the local branch of the National Trust and the Criterion Theatre. David was one of the founder members of the Friends of the Herbert Art Gallery and Museum, which recently folded after over thirty years. Ilse believes in a future of international harmony, (the only way forward) and of promoting understanding between different cultures and religions. Both she and David have joined a group of like-minded people, who meet once a month, working towards the same aim.

Their two children are now married and both have made music their career. Nicola lives in Edinburgh and Gavin and his family live locally. Despite their very active lives Ilse and David happily fulfil their role as grandparents to their son's two children.

Ilse was interviewed in June 2003

Miranda Aston.

'The muckier I got the more I liked it and I ended up with Swarfega (a grease remover used for hands) up to my elbows.' says Miranda Aston of her school holidays spent 'helping' in her father's garages.

Miranda was born to Pauline and Bill Aston in September 1960, at Friar's Craig Nursing Home in Coventry, the youngest of three girls. Her father was one of five brothers and after the war he set up in business, building a garage in Vecqueray Street, selling motorcycles. He eventually opened three more garages selling and maintaining motor vehicles, helped by his brothers and father-in-law. The family lived above one garage, but with the arrival of Miranda it became necessary to find larger living accommodation. Bill found a plot in Warwick Road, Coventry and using bricks from the old Coventry Railway Station built a house for his family.

Born into this engineering orientated family, at the age of five Miranda was given a child's tool kit which she still treasures and she has not looked back since. From the age of seven she began spending most of her school holidays with her father at his workplace 'helping' by checking the water, the oil and the screen wash. Working in the garage fascinated her. At the age of eight her father bought her a 'scrambler' bike which she loved riding over the fields when she was taken to watch the grass track motor cycle races.

Miranda always wanted to know how things worked. At home in the kitchen was what she describes as 'a lovely red timer clock with a white dial', which interested her to such an extent that she decided to find out how it worked. While her mother was in the garden one day, Miranda removed the back from the clock and began to undo one or two screws when it appeared to explode sending the parts across the kitchen. This gave her such a fright that she quickly retrieved the workings, pushed them back inside the clock, and screwed the back on. Strangely it never worked again!

Miranda's schooling began at Stoke Lodge School, a private establishment, which her two sisters, Paulette and Maxine also attended. Her father was keen for all his daughters to work in his businesses and the two older girls were taken away from the school at fifteen to do so. Fortunately for Miranda she passed the 'eleven plus' examination. She chose to attend Barrs Hill Grammar School for Girls, the reason being she preferred their blue uniform, rather than the red one as worn at Stoke Park, although she found wearing the beret embarrassing. Both schools later became comprehensive. The Head Teacher at Barrs Hill, Miss Melhuish, introduced herself to the new intake and shook the hands of each girl. This impressed Miranda and she loved her early years there taking a great pride in her school, especially when all the pupils walked to Holy Trinity Church in Broadgate for the Annual School Service, where they sang the school song, Jerusalem.

In her fourth year, Miranda was interviewed, concerning her future career and said she wanted to be an engineer. She was told 'You can't possibly do that, girls don't really do that' and alternatives were suggested more suitable for a Grammar School pupil! However, Miranda was adamant and 'stuck to her guns', a decision she has never regretted.

In the first year of her Ordinary (O-Level) exams, the grammar school became a comprehensive, and many of the staff whom Miranda knew well left, but she continued to progress and achieved exceptionally good examination results. Many of her friends also left at this stage and Miranda felt lonely as she began life in the sixth form studying for her Advanced (A-Level) exams in double maths and physics. She had chosen these subjects because of her determination to be an engineer. She disliked the maths finding them totally different from anything she had previously encountered at O-Level and says 'it was very hard. In the pure maths lessons we had seemed to stop using numbers and were working our way through the entire Greek alphabet! I just could not see the point of it or where it could be used'.

The seventies saw a revolution on the music scene with the advent of Punk, when many young people spiked their hair, wore torn clothes and stuck safety pins through their bodies. This new cult attracted Miranda and she embraced it fully, at the same time incurring the wrath of her teachers and the hostility of some pupils owing to her outrageous appearance, which saw her with white hair and wearing chains and safety pins everywhere. Understandably the school disapproved of Miranda turning up wearing such adornments. She faced being banned from the classroom and had to present herself to the head of the sixth form each morning for him to assess her suitability to attend classes. This made her feel even more rebellious. That and discovering her sexuality made school life even harder, especially when the school and fellow pupils found out. Sixth form life became very difficult for her and Miranda felt increasingly isolated. Therefore a combination of the A Level subjects, being lonely and becoming a punk, made it very difficult to go to school and she started to miss out on lessons. Eventually she virtually stopped going to school completely.

Miranda had been greatly attracted to the music produced by Punk Rock groups such as The Sex Pistols, the Slits, Siouxsie and the Banshees, The Au Pairs and especially The Passions who named an album *Michael and Miranda* after her. She enjoyed being part of a movement. 'Being punk was being me. One of the best things to come out of it was the Anti-Nazis Marches and Rock Against Racism. You felt you were changing the world'. Unfortunately, once the media latched on to the movement it changed and violence became synonymous with punk. Miranda's involvement then ceased.

An article in the *Daily Express* (7th February 1989), describing the Punk Movement, said 'they sent ripples of discontent through society'. The newspaper interviewed some previous members, including Miranda, all then holding responsible positions in business. They agreed unanimously that they had found the philosophy that 'anyone-can-do-anything' gave them confidence, an identity and most importantly they were part of a gang, outrageous though it was. Miranda says 'Dealing with hostility gave me a thick skin'. This was to prove necessary when she became the only woman on engineering courses.

However, the phase nearly cost her a career in engineering. In the preview to her A-Levels Miranda had been predicted to obtain marks in the eighties or nineties and on this basis she had received five offers of university places in London. She was also offered a sponsorship for 'quite a sizeable amount' from Lambeth Council, to study Civil Engineering. Unfortunately, as her personal problems increased and Miranda ceased to attend school, her mock A-Level results saw her marks plummet to twenty-six per cent. The shock of this led her to attempt to 'claw her way back', but time was short and even with her mum helping her to revise every night and supporting her, as she always did, her eventual results were disastrous; an E grade in physics, a fail in further maths and an 'O' grade in applied maths. Miranda did not know what she was going to do. From what had seemed to be a secure future now there did not appear to be one at all, in engineering at least. An apprenticeship was ruled out by age limits. She admits 'it was a scary, stressful time'. Nevertheless she pulled herself together and says 'I badgered the Careers Office in Coventry to such an extent that I practically lived there'.

The officer whom she admits she 'pestered to death' went through every possible career to do with engineering. He helped her considerably, putting letters together and writing all over the country. Fortunately one A-Level pass qualified a candidate to study for a Higher National Diploma (HND). The careers adviser suggested applying to the Lanchester Polytechnic, (now Coventry University) with a view to studying mechanical engineering. During her interview there Miranda was taken around the college and on seeing the Production Engineering laboratory she said 'That's the course I want to do, that's definitely the one I want to do'. Consequently she was offered a place, on condition that she found herself a factory willing to provide her with practical experience during vacations. This was a requirement for all sandwich courses, but it was August and getting close to the beginning of term.

Miranda wrote one hundred and twenty eight letters to employers asking for a sponsorship place, finally receiving a favourable reply from a Mr Lockhart, the Managing Director of Carbodies factory on the Holyhead Road (Now London Taxis International). He invited Miranda along for an interview. 'We chatted for over two hours. We got on like a house on fire'. Miranda still had white, 'punk' style hair, but wore smart clothes. Mr Lockhart said they had never had anyone apply for such a place, but they were willing to give her a chance. She says 'it was good to meet someone who judged you on your ability rather than on appearance'.

Arriving for her first ever taste of a manufacturing environment, Miranda went to see the Personnel Officer who did not quite know what to do with her. The firm made taxis from the initial piece of sheet metal to the complete vehicle, which was fairly unique. Miranda said that she would like to follow the production line from start to finish and it was suggested that she planned her own training. Thus she produced a draft itinerary which was accepted.

Miranda was given an overall and was put to work on a fly press. She had never been in a factory in her life and they had never, as far as she knew, had a girl doing such work. She worked for a week covertly watching the male operatives who were also watching her. As Miranda says 'they did not know what to make of me and I did not know what to make of them. It was a difficult situation for them added to which they were on 'piece work'. At the end of the week a worker from the 'Body in White' section approached her and asked if she would like to join them during their tea break. The ice was broken. From then on things went well except whilst making her own tool kit, as everyone had to do, she nearly knocked herself unconscious using the fly press! Later Miranda was to set a precedent when, on completion of her training, she returned to the firm as the only female production engineer at Carbodies'.

The change from school to further education was immense and Miranda welcomed being treated as an adult with the result she threw herself into the course with enthusiasm. Her results at the end of her first year at the polytechnic were up into the seventies and eighties [per cent] and by the end of the course she had gained five distinctions. She attributed her success to the relaxed atmosphere at the Lanchester and its mature attitude to students. Undoubtedly her enthusiasm and diligence also played a part.

Obtaining the HND qualification, and having had practical work experience at Carbodies, Miranda obtained a scholarship to Cranfield Institute of Technology. Bypassing a first degree, she spent two years studying for a Master of Science degree in Industrial Engineering and Production Management.

Miranda acknowledges that studying at Cranfield was the hardest work she had ever encountered in her life. Each day she had lectures and tutorials from nine until five except for Wednesday sports afternoons when the other students would play rugby. There were no other women on her course. She estimates that for every hour of written work one needed to work at least another one and a half hours outside the lesson. This went on relentlessly. Approximately thirty-six exams were taken each year, failure in any meant either a re-take or, in certain subjects, removal from the course. It was arduous, but Miranda credits it as being one of the best foundations in engineering she could ever have had. She had also set a precedent being the only woman to study production engineering there at that time. Nevertheless this did not stop the following item from appearing in the Cranfield newspaper 'the meeting agreed to the idea of inviting "old boys" to Steering Panel meetings and the Dinner afterwards'!

After Cranfield Miranda returned to Carbodies, but found it had changed, as she herself had now that she was a fully qualified engineer. She found the transition from studying a wide range of engineering topics to the world of work, where one seemed to specialise, was difficult. Soon she successfully applied to work for Jaguar Cars Limited, thus fulfilling one of her ambitions.

When one of the first Computer Numerically Controlled (CNC) machines was delivered to the Jaguar factory Miranda was one of the few engineers capable of doing the necessary programming. Her work now involves Computer Aided Design and Computer Aided Manufacturing (CAD/CAM) in fact everything necessary towards producing prototype parts and tools. She has worked at Jaguar cars for eighteen years and is now a Project Engineer. Owing to the secrecy of her present occupation the work is carried out in a windowless office and she says she 'would like to see the weather sometimes'.

In 1985 Miranda was extremely pleased to receive a letter from Mr Roger Binns, who had been the Deputy Head of Barrs Hill School during her punk era. It was he who had had the task of informing her of her disastrous A-level results. He wrote saying 'I did always believe that you would "win through" in the end ... "it really made my day" to hear just how well you have done. Congratulations'.

Miranda is a talented, energetic and determined role model and she joined the Women's Engineering Society (WES) and worked with them to encourage women to become engineers. She spoke to schoolgirls advising them on the importance of being determined and to 'just go for it'. For the Careers Office in Coventry, to whom she owed so much, Miranda joined a panel of guests for a 'What's my Line' game to raise the issue of equality of opportunity in the world of work. When she had started training only half to one per cent of engineering trainees were women, now the number has increased to about ten per cent. Unfortunately job prospects for either sex are not good, with so many factories closing, added to which engineering courses are not seen as popular. Nevertheless, it is a useful discipline to study.

In a letter to the WES Miranda wrote 'Being the only female at Cranfield was not all bad because the students came from various backgrounds and countries which led to some interesting discussions'. Neither did being the only female among a hundred students present problems.

If you can show that you know your subject, are keen and have the enthusiasm, people will take you at face value. I don't think I have ever come across resistance or problems. I think I was quite lucky, but you do have to have a thick skin and the ability to talk to all types of people from those on the shop floor to the managing director.

In 1988, following an article in the WES Miranda's name was put forward to enter a competition in *Cosmopolitan* magazine to find 'The Woman of Tomorrow'. This was to find a woman whose ambitions or achievements made her most likely to succeed. The judges were Anita Roddick of Body Shop fame, the fashion designer Betty Jackson and the television personality, Ruby Wax. A champagne breakfast at the Hyde Park Hotel in Knightsbridge preceded the finals of the competition. Miranda was one of ten women finalists in the Industry and Commerce category and finished runner up.

As a token of his pride Miranda's father presented her with a very large trophy and said how very proud he and her mother were. Initially he had regretted the fact that Miranda had not elected to work in his garage. He did not think one needed education, because he had run a successful business without it, but times had changed and Miranda was pleased to have gone on to grammar school. In contrast neither of her sisters became involved in engineering despite working in the garages. The reason for this according to Miranda is that 'they weren't dipping their arms in Swarfega, that's the trick!'

Miranda became disenchanted with the WES and wrote cancelling her membership. She felt that they were too pro-nuclear and pro-military at the time, whereas her concerns lay with environmental issues. If she was just starting her career Miranda says she would most likely study environmental engineering, a subject not on any curriculum when she went to the polytechnic. In her present occupation she does concern herself with the environment as much as possible. Working at the Jaguar's Whitley site, part of her responsibility is to look after their commitment to the environment and although fully involved in the project it has not yet been possible to turn the occupation into a full time one. It is carried out alongside her other work.

If the first of Miranda's ambitions was to work for the Jaguar the second was to become a Chartered Engineer. Once she had acquired a degree, spent two years on work experience and two years holding down a full-time position of responsibility, this ambition too was realised. Thus, from the 'out of control' punk rocker, Miranda Aston can now proudly write after her name M.Sc. C. Eng. M.I. Prod.E.

When Miranda had passed her driving test at seventeen her father bought her a Triumph Dolomite car, but forbade her to take it on the road until she was proficient at maintaining it and changing a wheel. Using a *Ladybird* book about cars as a start, she soon mastered the skill. Several years later she was approached by an adult education tutor at Barr's Hill school and asked if she could teach car maintenance, since she was an engineer. Miranda pointed out that she was not a mechanic, but the idea aroused interest. Together with her partner Ulli, she enrolled on a City and Guilds course in Light and Heavy Vehicle Maintenance. During this course they had to suffer what Miranda described as the worst lesson she had ever sat through, 'looking at thirty-four different clutch plates'. As usual the class consisted of males, most aged sixteen and seventeen, but the two mature candidates completed and passed the course with distinctions. This resulted in their teaching on an Adult Education Course.

The two taught car maintenance skills to women at various schools and colleges across Coventry, usually on a Saturday. They also produced a booklet to accompany the course. It was a 'hands on' course and pupils were set eight assignments which included changing wheels, oil, coolant and spark plugs. The tasks were written down on separate pieces of paper, to be drawn from a hat, and the women worked in pairs at their specific project. The courses were extremely popular and although it was hard work running the classes, it was most rewarding, seeing women become proficient in the necessary skills. The women practised these tasks on Miranda's Triumph

Dolomite, a car built in 1979, which was beginning to bear little resemblance to modern cars. Miranda joked that if her car did not start at the end of the training day they would all have to stay behind! The couple estimate the number of women taught car maintenance over six years as over seven hundred. The lessons ceased in the nineties, as car designs became more sophisticated and reliable, making it difficult for a layperson to access the workings. Miranda leads a very full life. In 1982 together with a group of friends she drove a white Cadillac 3,500 miles in the USA from San Francisco to New York via Chicago. This was under the Driveaway Scheme under which people paid to have their car taken from one place to another so it was waiting for them when they arrived to collect it.

In 1989 Miranda's father died, which made her reflect on her life, and she and Ulli decided that they should live life to the full while able. At school she had been very involved in all sports, but stopped participating when A-levels began and a more interesting social life took over. They both attended an Outward Bound course gaining skills in erecting tents, scuba diving, climbing, abseiling, canoeing and orienteering. The pair had no idea what this latter one was, but soon found out. They were given a map, an orange plastic cagoule and had to follow a route from point to point. It was pouring with rain and the map became soggier and soggier, but says Miranda 'we had the most wonderful time'. They are now keen members of the only orienteering group in Coventry, the Octavian Droobers, which had originated at Henry the Eighth school. In fact they now edit the magazine.

Some of Miranda's colleagues at the Jaguar invited her to take part in a charity walk. She accepted, admitting that she never walked any distance. She asked Ulli to accompany her, not knowing quite what she had let them both in for. The walk was across the Yorkshire Moors and was called the Lyke Wake Walk, a distance of forty-three miles from Osmotherly to Ravenscar. As a preliminary to the walk, the team drove to Wales and climbed up Snowdon twice in one day. The Lyke Wake Walk took sixteen hours and raised £1500 for the cancer ward at Walsgrave Hospital. This was particularly satisfying for Miranda for her father had received treatment there.

'We never looked back from then on' says Miranda. With Ulli she has run two London Marathons and the 'Coventry Way' a forty-mile circular trail, run or walked around the city, virtually all cross-country and including 125 stiles or gates. In this they held the Women's Record for three years. The route is now included on ordnance survey maps. They also developed an interest in cycling and took part in the London to Brighton cycle ride raising money for The British Heart Foundation. More recently they have taken up mountain bike orienteering and adventure racing.

To travel to every country is another ambition. So far Borneo and Peru are among countries visited and Miranda and Ulli went to Finland earlier this year [2003], where they took part in a husky dog safari enjoying it immensely, enough to plan a return visit. The list of prospective venues is endless and conservation work abroad now beckons. 'We have decided to do everything we can while we are able. If I get to be Prime Minister my policy would be to let people retire early and return to work later if they want. This would enable them to fulfil ambitions while they are young and fit'.

Sometimes events, which change one's life are for the best. Had Miranda passed her A-levels she would most likely have taken the offer from Lambeth and much of their civil engineering work involves working in sewers. On reflection she says 'I was probably spared a fate worse than death, so I think it's a good job I failed my A-Levels!' She also says that she would not have met her partner of twenty years, Ulli. In an interview given to *Coventry Jobhunter* (August 1985) Miranda said 'it's really worked out better than my original plans would have done. I realise that I'm enjoying production engineering more than I would have civil engineering'.

Finally Miranda says of her work 'with honesty I have never, ever been bored'.

Miranda was interviewed in March 2003.

~~~~~~~~~~~~~~~~~~~~~~~~~~~~~